Life on a Plate
The Journey of an Unlikely Chef

Sid Owen
with Martin Gray

Published by Century 2007

2 4 6 8 10 9 7 5 3 1

Copyright © Sid Owen 2007

Sid Owen has asserted his right under the Copyright, Designs
and Patents Act 1988 to be identified as the author of this work

First published in Great Britain in 2007 by
Century
Random House, 20 Vauxhall Bridge Road,
London SW1V 2SA

www.randomhouse.co.uk

Addresses for companies within The Random House Group
Limited can be found at:
www.randomhouse.co.uk

The Random House Group Limited Reg. No. 954009

A CIP catalogue record for this book
is available from the British Library

ISBN 9781846051739

The Random House Group Limited makes every effort to ensure
that the papers used in its books are made from trees that have
been legally sourced from well-managed and credibly certified
forests. Our paper procurement policy can be found at:
www.randomhouse.co.uk/paper.htm

Printed and bound by Firmengruppe APPL, aprinta druck,
Wemding, Germany

Photography by Martin Gray
Book designed by dave crook

acknowledgements

Sincere thanks are due to a great many people, for their help and support, and for encouraging my love of food and cooking.

Thanks firstly to my brothers Scott and Darren. Thank you to my agent Sandra Boyce, to Carol Mackie, Rosie P, Peter Begg, Jered Bolton, Emma Biggins and to Martin Gray for developing the book with me and for all the great pictures – I couldn't have done it without you mate.

Thank you to Dave Crook, Cathy Temple, Brice Maitre, Alan McJannet and to Louise Campbell, Katie Duce, Rob Waddington and my editor Hannah Black at Century.

Thanks to Simon, Clara and family, the Wooders, Mario and family, Jamie and the Wood family, Mel, Jason Kew, Geoff, Nick and Rachel Berry, Mariel, Amanda, John, Mitch, Mehmet, Chucky Star and all the guys at Chapel Market.

And finally, a big thank you to David, Gina, Danielle Petet and all my French colleagues and neighbours who helped make the restuarant a success – for making me so welcome.

a note about the recipes

The recipes in this book have been graded to give you an idea of how easy
or tricky they are. Don't be put off, none of the recipes are that difficult.
The following symbols are used throughout:

    ✳ simple

    ✳✳ a bit harder

    ✳✳✳ have a go

CHATEAU
Marie Plaisance
2003
BERGERAC SEC
APPELLATION BERGERAC SEC
ALAIN MERILLIER
PROPRIÉTAIRE À GAGEAC ROUILLAC
DORDOGNE - FRANCE
MIS EN BOUTEILLE AU
13,5% vol.
PRODUIT DE FRANCE

contents

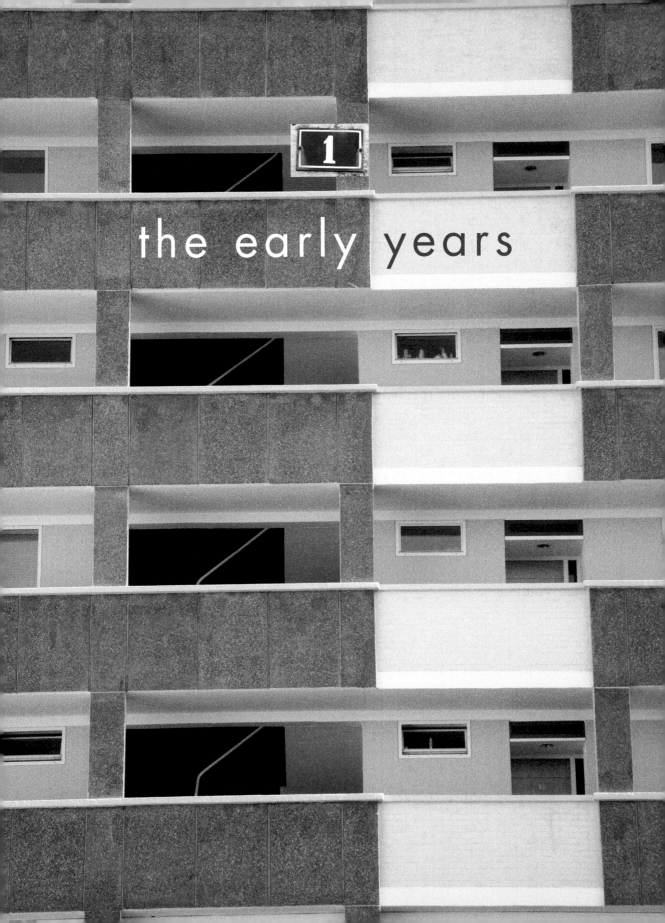

1

the early years

I was born on an estate, slap bang in the middle of Chapel Market in north London, the youngest of four boys. Many of my earliest memories involve the market. We were a local family and friendly with a lot of the people who worked there. We were part of the community, and the market was right in the heart of it. For us kids, it was kind of like a big playground. Everyone knew me and my brothers. I'm

not saying we were little angels, we weren't, and like a lot of boys we'd get into fights and all sorts, but my mum knew the traders would look out for us.

Things were a bit rough and ready, and people didn't get too fussed over the odd bit of bother here and there. In fact, many of the traders were very kind. There was one guy who'd give me and my brothers a carrot every single day. A raw carrot, and we'd eat it on the street like a lollipop. We couldn't afford sweets, but this was miles better for the teeth.

Like a lot of local families, we kinda lived from hand to mouth, particularly in our case with Mum being a single parent with four growing boys to look after. It really helped being part of a tight-knit community – the traders knew we didn't have a lot of money, so they'd give us a bit extra, or any leftover fruit and veg they had to spare. We'd take it back to Mum, and

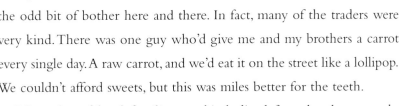

she'd make something with it. In many ways, we didn't have that bad a diet. It was all based on basic, healthy ingredients – fruit and veg and, as often as possible, meat from the butcher. No fancy cuts or anything, but my mum knew how to make a good

stew with any kind of meat. I remember the smell of the long, slow cooking, and I loved the way the vegetables would soak up all the flavours and juices of the meat. It was drummed into us: eat carrots and you'll be able to see in the dark, eat your greens so your hair goes curly – all these little myths would stick in your mind. Like most kids, I wasn't that big on vegetables then, but I always liked them in a good stew. To this day, even though I don't make stews that often, they still remind me of being all warm and cosy and among family and friends.

My mum was anything but a fancy cook. Left on her own with four boys to keep under control, there wasn't exactly time for experimenting in the kitchen or money for posh stuff, but she knew how to take what was available and make it into something tasty and filling. Back then, packaged food was sold more as a luxury item and was something we never had.

Beef or lamb stew

This dish always warms my cockles during the winter months.

Serves 4 to 6

olive oil

600g stewing beef or lamb, off the bone and cut into cubes

plain flour for dusting

2 medium onions, peeled and sliced

2 cloves of garlic, peeled and crushed

salt and freshly ground black pepper

1 glass of red wine (optional)

1 litre beef or lamb stock

Worcestershire sauce

a sprig of fresh thyme, leaves picked

4 potatoes, peeled and cut into chunks

4 carrots, peeled and cut into chunks

2 small turnips, scrubbed and cut into chunks

2 parsnips, peeled and cut into chunks

2 bay leaves

a handful of button mushrooms, wiped and trimmed

tomato purée

Heat a large, heavy frying pan and add a good splash of olive oil. Toss your chunks of beef or lamb in a little flour so it's nice and evenly covered before you cook it, this helps seal the meat and gives your sauce a nice thick consistency. Fry the meat quickly in the hot pan on all sides, then add your sliced onion and garlic and season well with salt and pepper.

Tip the meat, onions and garlic into a stewing pot or saucepan big enough to hold all your ingredients. Rinse the frying pan out with a glass of red wine or a little of the stock, making sure you get all the lovely sticky bits off the bottom, and add to the pot. Pour in the rest of the stock, add a couple of dashes of Worcestershire sauce and the thyme, and bring to the boil.

Turn the heat down to medium and add the potatoes, carrots, turnips and parsnips. Simmer for about half an hour, then add your bay leaves and mushrooms. Keep stirring now and then, making sure nothing sticks to the bottom of the pot, topping the level of liquid up if it starts to get low. Add a squeeze of tomato purée, stir, and cook for another 45 minutes to an hour, tasting and seasoning all the time, until all the veg is cooked and the meat falls apart and melts in your mouth.

Lamb chops with garlic, rosemary, thyme and sautéd potatoes

Serves 2

6 thick juicy lamb chops

1 clove of garlic, peeled and crushed

a sprig of fresh thyme, leaves picked

a sprig of fresh rosemary, leaves picked

salt and freshly ground black pepper

olive oil

500g potatoes, peeled

Preheat your oven to 200°C/400°F/gas mark 6.

Put your lamb chops into a dish with the crushed garlic, herbs, plenty of salt and pepper and a good drizzle of olive oil. Leave to marinate for about half an hour.

Put your spuds into a saucepan full of cold salted water, then put on the heat, bring to the boil and simmer until almost cooked. Drain and slice thickly.

Heat a heavy ovenproof frying pan. Take your chops out of their marinade and fry them for about 3 minutes on each side. Place the pan in the oven with the chops in it, and pan-roast them for about 10 minutes. Lift the chops out of the pan with a set of tongs, place them on a plate and keep warm.

Put the pan back on the heat with the lamb fat and juices still in it. Add a splash of olive oil and the sliced potatoes. Sauté the potatoes in the fat, for 10 minutes or so, until nice and brown and crisp. Serve the lamb chops with the crispy sauté potatoes and some aubergine and courgette ratatouille (page 269).

Cottage pie

Serves 4 to 6

    1 onion, peeled and finely chopped

    1 clove of garlic, peeled and chopped

    750g minced beef

    Worcestershire sauce

    1 glass of red wine

    balsamic vinegar

    2 carrots, peeled and finely chopped

    a sprig of fresh rosemary

    1 beef stock cube

    tomato purée

    1kg potatoes

    a knob of butter

    3 handfuls of frozen peas

    1 tomato, cut into pieces

    2 handfuls of grated Cheddar cheese

    salt and freshly ground black pepper

Preheat your oven to 200°C/400°F/gas mark 6.

In a saucepan, brown the onion, garlic and beef over a medium heat. Add a good dash of Worcestershire sauce, the wine and a glug of balsamic vinegar. Carry on cooking for 5 minutes, then add the chopped carrots and the rosemary sprig.

In a separate saucepan, boil 300ml of water with the stock

cube and a good squeeze of tomato purée. Add the stock to the meat pan little by little to keep the mince moist as it cooks.

Peel the potatoes, put them into a deep saucepan and cover with water. Add a pinch of salt and bring to the boil, then turn the heat down to a simmer. When your potatoes are done, drain them in a colander and mash them with a good knob of butter and plenty of salt and pepper.

When the mince has been simmering for half an hour, add the peas and cook for about 5 minutes more. Taste the mince and add more salt and pepper if you need to, then pour into a baking dish. Fork the mash over the top of the mince, keeping it rough as this helps it crisp up. Scatter with the chopped tomato and grated cheese and place in the hot oven for 15 minutes, until the cottage pie is bubbling hot and the top is crispy and browned.

Baked sardines with lemon and parsley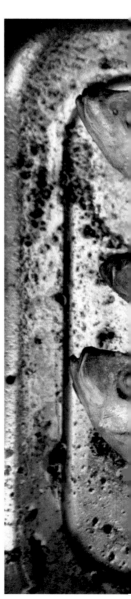

These sardines can work either as a starter or as a main, with tapas, olives, cured meats and crusty bread.

Serves 4

8 fresh whole sardines, gutted and cleaned

1 lemon

olive oil

salt and freshly ground black pepper

a small bunch of fresh flat-leaf parsley, leaves picked

Preheat your oven to 180°C/350°F/gas mark 4.

First, if you're not sure how to gut and clean your sardines, ask your fishmonger to do it for you! Pat them dry with some kitchen paper and lay them on a baking tray. Slice half the lemon into wedges and place one wedge inside each fish. Squeeze the remaining half of the lemon over the fish and drizzle well with olive oil. Sprinkle with lots of salt and pepper and cook in the preheated oven for 15 minutes.

While the sardines are cooking, chop your parsley finely. When they're ready, sprinkle the parsley all over the sardines and serve.

Tagliatelle bolognese

Serves 4

  olive oil

  1 onion, peeled and finely chopped

  1 clove of garlic, peeled and chopped

  a few sprigs of fresh thyme, leaves picked

  1kg minced beef, or a mixture or beef and pork

  salt and freshly ground black pepper

  1 teaspoon of balsamic vinegar

  1 glass of red wine

  2 small carrots, finely chopped

  2 x 400g tins of plum tomatoes

  a handful of mushrooms, cleaned and sliced

  a small bunch of fresh basil, leaves picked

  a squeeze of tomato purée or ketchup

  500g fresh tagliatelle

  grated Parmesan cheese to serve

Heat a large saucepan, pour in a splash of olive oil and add the onion, garlic and thyme. Add your mince, season well with salt and pepper, and cook until it starts to brown. Add the balsamic vinegar to keep it moist and tenderize it a bit, and then the wine. Add the carrots and any other chopped vegetables you feel like using, then all your tomatoes.

Bring to the boil and simmer for about 10 minutes, then add the mushrooms, half the basil leaves and the tomato purée. Keep simmering for about another 20 minutes, stirring now and again to make sure nothing sticks to the bottom of the pan.

Cook the pasta according to the packet instructions, then drain in a colander and divide between four plates. Season the sauce with a little salt and pepper and serve sprinkled with the rest of the basil leaves and the Parmesan.

Leek and potato soup ☀

Serves 4 to 6

> 2 big potatoes, peeled and diced
>
> 2 leeks
>
> a good knob of butter
>
> a litre of chicken stock
>
> salt and freshly ground black pepper
>
> 3 tablespoons single cream
>
> a few sprigs of fresh flat-leaf parsley (optional)

Place the potatoes in a saucepan, cover with salted water and bring to the boil. Simmer for 5 minutes, then drain well.

Trim any rough-looking leaves off the outside of the leeks and trim off the tops and the roots. Slice the leeks down the middle and then cut across into chunks. Wash carefully in a colander under cold running water to make sure you get rid of any dirt, and drain.

Melt the butter in a deep saucepan, add the leeks and cook slowly for about 10 minutes, until soft. Add the parboiled potatoes, and cook together for another 5 minutes, then adding the stock and bring to the boil. Season to taste with salt and pepper, simmer until the potatoes are cooked and soft, then blitz with a stick blender until smooth.

Place the soup back on the heat and add the cream. Cook for a couple more minutes, then ladle the soup into bowls and serve with a twist of pepper and a sprig of parsley.

Mixed veg side dish

This dish goes great with most meat and fish dishes and is easy and quick to rustle up.

Serves 4

    salt and freshly ground black pepper

    200g green beans

    olive oil

    2 cloves of garlic, peeled and finely chopped

    1 red onion, peeled and roughly chopped

    2 medium courgettes, sliced

    10 cherry tomatoes, cut in half

Bring a large saucepan of salted water to the boil. Trim the tops and tails off your green beans, then drop them into the boiling water and simmer for about 5 minutes. Drain in a colander and put to one side.

Heat a non-stick wok or frying pan and add a good glug of oil, the garlic, onion and courgettes. Fry on a medium heat for a few minutes until everything starts to soften, then season well with salt and pepper. Add the tomatoes and the green beans and cook for 5 minutes more. Taste, season with more salt and pepper if you need to, and serve.

For a treat, we'd have fish and chips on a Friday – that would save my mum cooking – and we'd go to the pie and mash shop on a Saturday. These were both favourites, partly because they were cheap. You could get a good meal for next to nothing; pie and mash was only a pound then, probably less. Our local pie and mash shop was a bit of an institution and hadn't changed since Victorian times. Even to this day it looks exactly the same. In fact, now it's Grade II listed as a bit of Old London. It's a long narrow shop – rows and rows of booths, plain wooden benches and marble tables with wrought-iron legs. It's got black and white tiled floors and walls, everything plain but spotless.

They'd make up hundreds of pies at a time. The pastry would be rolled out at the back of the shop and pushed into giant pie trays, then filled with mince, covered with pastry lids and baked in huge ovens. The finished pies would be brought out front and kept in hot trays. Beside them was a huge vat of mashed potato and another of liquor (a kind of tangy parsley gravy). The punters would stand in a queue and a quick production line of meals would be plated up. Pie, mash, liquor. Slap, bang, wallop. Me and my brothers used to stand in the queue behind Mum and peer over and watch it all being done, our mouths watering. I loved the smell and the friendly hustle and bustle of it all. Everyone knew the owners and we'd always bump into neighbours and the like.

But as I say, that was a treat. On a day-to-day basis, you just mixed and matched your meat, veg and potatoes. Whether it was chops or stew, it was always meat, veg and potatoes. That was your diet.

It worries me that so many kids are now growing up on packaged food. It's getting cheaper and cheaper, so people who don't have a lot of money buy it because it seems to cost less than your veg. But often the costs are cut by processing the food in a way that removes a lot of the goodness. It's also often pumped full of salt, sugar and fat as a cheap way of making it taste good.

When you think about it, if you've got a family to feed, or even if you're on your own, you can make larger amounts with your basic ingredients and freeze what's left. So although packaged foods seem cheap, they can be a false economy, because they only stretch to one meal. Kids are always going to like your pizzas, your burgers, and all that kind of thing, and it doesn't do them any harm to have this sort of stuff as a treat, but for more and more kids, that's all they're getting. It's tempting for mums and dads to buy food they know their children will eat. If you've got to be careful about what you're spending, and you cook them something and they won't eat it, you panic, because you don't want them to go hungry. But I'm hoping that you'll find in these pages some

good, wholesome recipes that aren't expensive or complicated to make and that you, your family, kids and friends will really love.

When I was about seven, my mother became very ill. Me and my brothers didn't quite know what was wrong for a while, but she had been diagnosed with cancer. My mum died six months later. It was a difficult time for the family, with people deciding where we boys should go. My oldest brother was a lot older, and moved away by himself. Darren was sent to another relative, and me and my brother Scott stayed in various places over the following months and years and for a while we went to live with my mum's sister and her husband , still in Islington.

They were keen cooks and had done quite well for themselves so could afford to spend a bit more on ingredients. I'm not saying that experimenting with food should rely on money, but it made more things available. They would buy really good produce – they shopped in places we'd barely been inside before, like the food halls of department stores. Buying in proper good meat and different kinds of fish.

Scott and I were always in the kitchen – we were intrigued by what went on there and liked to watch my aunt's husband prepare the meals. He was the cook of the house, and was passionate about food. His obvious enjoyment of cooking encouraged us to think differently about it. We now had the chance to try different food, like pasta and salads and fish you actually cooked at home. Until then the

only fish I'd eat came from the fish and chip shop.

We always had a Sunday roast, and we were encouraged to be healthier, and try different vegetables. I was taking it all in, the new ingredients, the new tastes and I'd think: It's not that difficult, really.

From an early age, I suppose I've always thought of food as being more than something that just sits in front of you on the plate to be eaten – which is probably not so normal for a child. Being around my aunt and her husband, who were such keen cooks, had an impact and I think that in an attempt to form a connection of some kind with them I was keen to learn more about food and cooking.

The first chance I got to put what I'd learnt into practice was in a cooking class in Penton Primary School when I was ten. I had never heard of quiche before, but I cooked one in the class. I really enjoyed the cooking lesson and taking the quiche home. I was so proud of it, I brought it home from school and laid it on the table and said, 'Yeah, I made that.' At that age, if kids want a sandwich, they ask their mum, but me and Scott would fend for ourselves. We started making our own sandwiches, and we would always try and push it a little bit further. 'What if we put this in the sandwich?' So I suppose it started from ten upwards, really.

Peasants' pasta

This recipe is very versatile – use dried herbs (mixed) if you don't have any thyme, and passata if you don't have any cherry tomatoes. Cook a bit more pasta and the sauce will stretch to 4 people.

Serves 2

olive oil

4 rashers of bacon, chopped

1 onion, peeled and finely chopped

2 cloves of garlic, peeled and chopped

a few sprigs of fresh thyme, leaves picked

salt and freshly ground black pepper

500g cherry tomatoes, cut in half

a squeeze of tomato purée or ketchup

crushed chillies (optional)

a small bunch of basil, leaves picked

2 tablespoons crème fraiche or single cream (optional)

250g dried penne

grated Parmesan cheese to serve

Heat a large saucepan and add a splash of olive oil. Fry the bacon, onion, garlic and thyme for a few minutes, until softened and lightly browned. Season with a bit of pepper, but no salt, as the bacon's already quite salty. Add the tomatoes, tomato purée and some crushed chillies if you fancy giving the flavour a bit of a kick, and cook for about 10 minutes, until the tomatoes have cooked down and turned into a sauce. Keep stirring to make sure nothing sticks. Add the basil leaves and a little crème fraiche if you want to take the edge off the sauce, and cook for a couple more minutes.

Cook the pasta according to the packet instructions and drain in a colander. Stir into the sauce, season with a little salt and pepper, and serve sprinkled with Parmesan.

Courgette and broccoli cheese bake

Serves 4 to 6

> 1 tablespoon butter
>
> 2 tablespoons plain flour
>
> 300ml organic skimmed milk
>
> 2 handfuls of grated cheese – Cheddar and double Gloucester are good
>
> 1 teaspoonful grain or English mustard
>
> salt and freshly ground black pepper
>
> 4 medium courgettes, cut into big chunks
>
> 1 head of broccoli, cut into chunky florets

Preheat your oven to 200°C/400°F/gas mark 6.

Melt the butter in a saucepan over a low heat. Add the flour and stir with a wooden spoon until you have a smooth paste. Pour in the milk, stirring all the time, then bring to the boil and when the sauce thickens a little, stir in the cheese and the mustard. When all the cheese has melted into the sauce, season with salt and pepper and keep warm.

Bring a large saucepan of salted water to the boil. Cook your courgettes for 2 minutes, then fish them out with a slotted spoon, leave them to drain in a colander and do the same with your broccoli. Lay the veg in an ovenproof baking dish and pour the warm cheese sauce over the top.

Place the baking dish in the preheated oven and bake for about 20 minutes, until hot through and bubbling brown on top.

Sid's easy-peasy all-season oven-baked mackerel ☀

This is a simple, cheap and cheerful snack I used to cook for myself when I wanted something quick but tasty and healthy. Two small pieces of mackerel are normally enough for one person.

Serves 2

> 4 pieces of smoked mackerel
>
> white wine vinegar

Preheat your oven to 180°C/350°F/gas mark 4.

Take the smoked mackerel out of the packet and place it on a tray in the preheated oven for no longer than 10 minutes. It's quite oily, so there's no need to add oil or butter to keep it moist. When it comes out of the oven, splash it with a little vinegar before you serve it.

In the summer it's brilliant with a bit of green salad, beetroot, coleslaw and potato salad, and in winter it's nice to serve it with mashed or sautéed potatoes with a little butter and rosemary and even pea purée (see page 238). Sometimes I fry a few rashers of bacon until they're starting to get crispy and lay the rashers over the mackerel before I put it into the oven. This gives the fish an even smokier flavour, and it works really well with mashed potato and sweetcorn (see page 44).

Fisherman's pie

This is a classic dish, great served with my mixed veg side dish (see page 29).

Serves 4 to 6

> 500g skinless salmon fillet, cut into chunks
>
> 500g skinless cod fillet, cut into chunks
>
> the juice of 1 lemon
>
> salt and freshly ground black pepper
>
> 1kg potatoes, peeled
>
> 4 eggs, in their shells
>
> a knob of butter
>
> 1 small clove of garlic, peeled and chopped
>
> 2 leeks, chopped, washed and drained
>
> 2 carrots, peeled and finely chopped
>
> 1 glass of white wine
>
> 180ml single cream
>
> 150g grated Cheddar cheese, plus more for topping
>
> 1 teaspoon English mustard
>
> a big handful of frozen peas
>
> a few sprigs of fresh flat-leaf parsley, chopped

Preheat your oven to 200°C/400°F/gas mark 6.

Get yourself a good-sized ovenproof baking dish and scatter the salmon and cod chunks evenly in the bottom of it. Drizzle the lemon juice over the fish, sprinkle with salt and pepper and put in the fridge while you prepare the other ingredients.

Place your potatoes and eggs in a saucepan, cover with cold water, bring to the boil and turn the heat down to a simmer. After about 8 more minutes, fish the eggs out and place them somewhere to cool. Keep boiling the potatoes until they're cooked through, then drain in a colander and put to one side.

Melt the butter in a small saucepan and add the garlic, leeks and carrots. Cook for 10 minutes or so, until they're a nice light golden brown, then add the wine and cook for another 5 minutes to evaporate the alcohol. In another saucepan, heat the cream with the Cheddar and mustard. When all the cheese has melted into the cream, stir in the frozen peas and the parsley. Tip the sauce on to the carrots and leeks, then pour the mixture over the fish in the baking dish. Shell the boiled eggs, cut them in quarters and arrange over the top.

Mash the potato, season it with salt and pepper and tip it out on to a clean work surface. Press it flat with your hands, then lift slabs of it up and lay it over the top of the pie filling. When you have a nice even topping of mash, sprinkle with some extra Cheddar (or Gruyère or Parmesan if you want a little more flavour) and bake the pie in the preheated oven for about 35 minutes. If the top isn't as golden brown as you'd like, you can put it under the grill to finish it off.

Fish stew

Serves 4

250g monkfish fillet

250g salmon fillet

250g cod fillet

12 large fresh raw prawns

500g potatoes, peeled and cut into chunks

2 small onions, peeled and sliced

2 sticks of celery, diced

2 cloves of garlic, peeled and chopped

1 small red pepper, deseeded and diced

a few sprigs of fresh flat-leaf parsley, leaves picked

a few sprigs of fresh tarragon, leaves picked and chopped

fish seasoning

salt and freshly ground black pepper

olive oil

juice of 1 lemon

600g mussels

12 cherry tomatoes, cut in half

1 big glass of white wine

1 x 400g can of chopped tomatoes

a good squeeze of tomato purée or ketchup

Trim the skin and any ragged bits off your fish and pick out any bones. Peel the prawns and put all the fish and prawn trimmings into a small saucepan. Prepare all your vegetables and add any trimmings to the pan too, including the stalks from the parsley and tarragon. Cover with about 275ml of water, bring to the boil and simmer gently for about 15 minutes. Pour through a sieve and keep to one side. This is your fish stock and it's going to make your stew taste brilliant.

Cut the fish into big chunks, lay out on a clean plate or tray and season well with fish seasoning, salt and pepper, a drizzle of olive oil and a squeeze of lemon. Cover, and place in the fridge to marinate for about an hour. Wash your mussels in plenty of cold water, pulling off any beardy bits you find on them, and throw away any that aren't tightly closed.

Place the potatoes in a saucepan, cover with cold salted water and bring to the boil. Simmer for 5 minutes until they're about half cooked, then drain in a colander and put to one side.

Heat a big saucepan or deep casserole, pour in a splash of olive oil and add your onions, celery, garlic, pepper, cherry tomatoes and most of the herbs. Cook gently for about 10 minutes, until soft, then add your wine and your parboiled potatoes cut into chunks. Let the alcohol evaporate for a few minutes, then add the tinned tomatoes, a good squeeze of tomato purée and your fish stock, and bring to the boil.

After the stew has been simmering for a few minutes, add the monkfish and give it a head start because it takes longer to cook than the other fish. After 5 minutes or so, add the salmon and cod, turn the heat right down to a simmer and put the lid on. Cook gently for another 7 minutes and finally add the prawns and mussels. Cover with a lid and cook for 5 minutes more, until the mussels have opened. Pick out any that haven't and throw them away. Sprinkle the stew with the remaining parsley and tarragon, and serve with plenty of nice crusty French bread.

Sweetcorn side ☀

Serves 4

    1 x 320g tin of sweetcorn, drained

    a few tablespoons skimmed milk

    a knob of butter

    salt and freshly ground black pepper

Empty the sweetcorn into a saucepan, add the milk and bring to the boil. Simmer until the sweetcorn is hot, stirring now and then to make sure nothing sticks. Stir in the butter, season with a little salt and pepper and serve.

Green pesto pasta salad ☀

You can make your own pesto, but there are some really good ones available in jars if you have a look around your local deli or supermarket.

Serves 4 to 6

400g farfalle 'butterfly' pasta

salt and freshly ground black pepper

4 tablespoons pesto

6 tablespoons mayonnaise

extra virgin olive oil

Parmesan cheese to serve

Cook the pasta in plenty of boiling salted water until it's just cooked but still has a little bite. Drain in a colander and rinse with cold water until cool. Shake the pasta around in the colander until completely drained and tip into the mixing bowl.

Spoon in the pesto, mayonnaise and olive oil and stir until the pasta is well coated with everything. Taste, and add a little salt and pepper if necessary, and a little more mayo if it's a bit dry.

Serve with another glug of olive oil over the top and a good sprinkling of Parmesan.

When I was about thirteen, we moved from Islington to Cockfosters, which is much further north. There was no pie and mash shop where we lived now, but about once a month, my aunt might say, 'Let's get some pie and mash.' She'd bring it home as a takeaway. We had it the traditional way, with the liquor.

I had started acting professionally at eight years of age. I'd always been interested in acting, for as long as I can remember. When I was about 5 I remember becoming a big fan of the Bugsy Malone film which had just been released. It really got me into the idea of children acting too. In the area where I grew up, the Anna Scher drama school was nearby, and I saw these kids coming in and out of the school and I was always intrigued. I was so inspired by what these kids were doing and by Bugsy Malone that when I was six or seven, I went in there and put my name down. I had to wait a year before I got in, and I went two evenings a week for 25 pence, (part of a scheme for poorer kids). By the time I was eight or nine I had started getting some professional acting jobs because I was spotted in one of the classes by the agent Sandra Boyce, who is still my agent to this day.

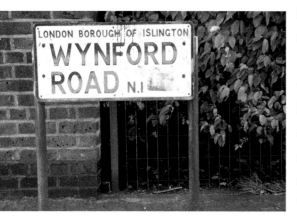

Even though I was gradually getting busier with the acting, I was still going home and having dinner with my relatives at night. The dramatic change came when I was thirteen and I got a big role in a feature film, playing alongside Al Pacino, as his son, in *Revolution*. This job took me away on location for a year, to different parts of England and abroad, and completely out of school. I was living in hotels with my tutor and chaperone. During the day, I would eat from film catering. Film catering is actually a lot better nowadays, but even then, compared to what I was used to as a kid, it was like a lavish buffet, with things I'd never tasted before. Apart from my wages, they would give me £200 a week in expenses. I'd never seen money like that before, so I really was like the kid in a sweet shop. We were eating in a hotel restaurant every night. At home, fish and chips from the chippy was a treat on a Saturday, but suddenly I could have whatever I wanted; so instead of having good wholesome home-cooked food, here were these menus with steak and chips, fish and chips – and, of course, like any child that age, that's what you'd want, so that's what you'd choose. I was out on my own, so I rebelled, eating rubbish – chips with everything and puddings every night. I remember one guy used to eat steak for breakfast, because he could.

Although I had a chaperone to look after me, there was no parental figure there to make sure I got my veg and didn't over-indulge. Having said that, on a job I'd done for a telly thing in the TV-am building in Camden, they actually stopped me eating sweets. I was going home and eating healthy food at night, but during the day, me and the other child actors were stuffing our faces with sweets. I was just crazy. Because we were so hyperactive, they stopped us eating sweets and would give us a bag at the end of the day instead.

After the film, it was hard for me to go back to my normal

secondary school, because my face was getting known on screen and it was difficult for me to blend in with the other kids. I'd made a bit of money from the film, and we decided, between my relatives and Sandra and myself, to use it to pay for my fees at an American International school. We looked at various schools and chose that one because there were kids from all different countries – Arabs, Americans, Scandinavians – and I thought I'd be able to melt into the background. The kids didn't know about my acting until they went on a class outing and went to see the film I was in – *Revolution*. It was part of their education, the American Revolution, so the class watched the film. That blew my cover.

But the kids I was now mixing with had very different backgrounds from my own. I'd been away for a year, not involved in cooking, and one thing that reignited my interest in food was that the school would have an international evening at the end of term. Everyone had to bring a dish from their own country. One thing that sticks in my mind is an Araby sort of stewy dish, with a bit of spice. I remember trying that. It was nice to try something different, and that was my first real taste of spicy food. I didn't know it at the time, but this was to be the start of a love of all things spicy. And you'll see that love in some of the recipes in this book.

When I was fourteen or fifteen, when I lived at Cockfosters, I got very friendly with a Greek Cypriot guy and I would eat at his house twice a week. We ate very traditional Cypriot dishes – Greek stews, soups and a lot of meat, a lot of lamb. My friend's mum, Mariel, was a great cook. She was passionate about her food. The Cypriot woman tends to stays home and cook, so she spent hours in the kitchen. I would go round for dinner and the smell would be unbelievable. Regardless of whether I had had dinner or not, Mariel would make something for me anyway, because she was proud – rice dishes, nice potatoes with coriander, lots of salads with onions mixed in and tomatoes, cucumbers, with mixed spicy seasoning. A Mediterranean mixture of ground spices you put on your salad. Lots of olive oil. And the bread was beautiful. You'd have hummus or aubergine dips, all that stuff. Great moussaka. A bit like lasagne or our shepherd's pie. The same produce I'd grown up with, but used differently, so this was all new to me.

Healthy hummus

Makes a nice bowlful

2 x 400g tins of chickpeas

2 cloves of garlic, crushed

4 tablespoons tahini paste

extra virgin olive oil

juice of 1 lemon

salt and freshly ground black pepper

Tip the chickpeas into a colander and drain well. Put them into a food processor and add the crushed garlic, tahini, a good few glugs of olive oil and the lemon juice. Blitz for a few seconds until smooth, then take the lid off and taste.

Season with salt and pepper and more lemon juice if you need to, and if the hummus is a bit dry, add a little water or a drop more oil and blitz again.

Serve with strips of toasted pitta bread and carrot sticks, or even with crisps as a snack or part of a mezze platter.

Aioli

    2 cloves of garlic, peeled

    salt

    1 small jar of mayonnaise

    lemon juice

Using a garlic press, crush the garlic into a small bowl and add the mayonnaise. Mix together and season with a little salt, pepper and a squeeze of lemon

Guacamole

Makes enough for 4

     2 large or 3 small soft ripe avocados

     1 clove of garlic, peeled

     ½ a red onion

     a small bunch of fresh coriander

     olive oil

     1 tablespoon of yoghurt or crème fraiche

     1 fresh red chilli

     salt and freshly ground black pepper

     1 fresh lime

     Tabasco sauce

With a small sharp knife, cut each avocado down to the stone as if you were trying to cut it in half lengthways. Twist the two halves so they come apart and you'll be left with one half with the stone in and the other without. Scoop the stone out with a spoon, then scoop the flesh out of its skin and place it in a mixing bowl. Keep the stones to one side.

When you've got all the avocado ready, chop the garlic and red onion as finely as you can and add to the mixing bowl with the chopped coriander. Add a good glug of olive oil and a spoonful of yoghurt or crème fraiche. Chop the chilli and add it too, but if you don't want your guacamole too hot, cut it in half lengthways first and scoop out the seeds with a teaspoon before you chop it. Season with salt and pepper, a good squeeze of lime and a couple of dashes of Tabasco to give it a bit of a bite.

Mash everything together with a fork or a potato masher and, for the best flavour, leave the guacamole for half an hour or so before serving. Place the avocado stones in the bowl with it and they'll stop it turning brown. Take out the stones before serving, and season with a little more salt and pepper and lime juice if you need to.

Serve with nachos, or sticks of fresh carrot and celery if you want to go for a healthier option.

2

discovering new
flavours

By the time I got to fifteen or sixteen, I'd left my unce and aunt's. My brother Scott had moved out a couple of years earlier and, since Mum's death, Darren had spent most of the time living above a pub not too far away. It ended up that we all needed somewhere to live at the same time, and it seemed a great opportunity for us to live together as a family again. Darren found a squat back in Islington, so Scott and I moved in with him. We were three teenage boys living together, almost right back where we lived before. It might sound a bit mad now, but it was easier to squat then – you could get electricity and running water quite easily. Me and Darren were in about three different squats over the next couple of years. The money I'd earned from *Revolution* was long gone at this point, what with school and everything. We were fending for ourselves, and back to trying to get food as cheaply as possible down the market. At that time, we could buy a whole bag of veg for peanuts, and

that encouraged us to cook. We had to look at the stuff we bought – touch it, feel it, work out if it was OK to eat and what we could do with it. How do you tell a bad onion? You have to squeeze the top. The same goes for garlic, you can tell by feeling. You'll know when a fruit is off, by the smell and the colour.

When we first started living together, Darren was like a father figure and he would be the one to cook. He'd lived at the pub for a long time, and they used to serve a lot of home-cooked food. He'd pitched in with the cooking, bottling up, all

sorts. Scott had had the same upbringing as I had, so although he and I were probably a bit more adventurous, Darren had that bit of culinary experience.

To start with, there wasn't much money, so we cooked because that was the only way we could eat well. But being back in Islington, we'd still go down the pie and mash shop on a Saturday and get our fish and chips on a Friday. Darren really loved cooking and his passion brushed off on to Scott and then on to me. He could do good traditional English dishes like sausages and mash and onion gravy, and steak and chips: the stuff he'd learned in the pub. Then Scott started learning to cook, then I pitched in as well. I was already very interested in food, and now I got the chance to start learning.

Sid's good old British bangers, parsnip mash and onion gravy

This is nice served with baby carrots, peas and Dijon or English mustard.

Serves 4

500g potatoes, chopped

500g parsnips, chopped

salt and freshly ground black pepper

8 sausages

olive oil

a knob of butter

2–3 tablespoons single cream or low-fat milk

2 onions, peeled and thinly sliced

a glass or two of red wine

1 vegetable stock cube

1 teaspoon Marmite

a squeeze of tomato purée or tomato ketchup

1 tablespoon plain flour, sifted

Preheat your oven to 200°C/400°F/gas mark 6.

Peel the potatoes and parsnips, place them in a deep saucepan and cover them with water. Add a pinch of salt and bring to the boil, then turn the heat down to a simmer.

Sear your sausages in a hot frying pan with a splash of oil, and when browned on all sides, tip them on to a baking tray and place in the preheated oven. Cook them for about 20

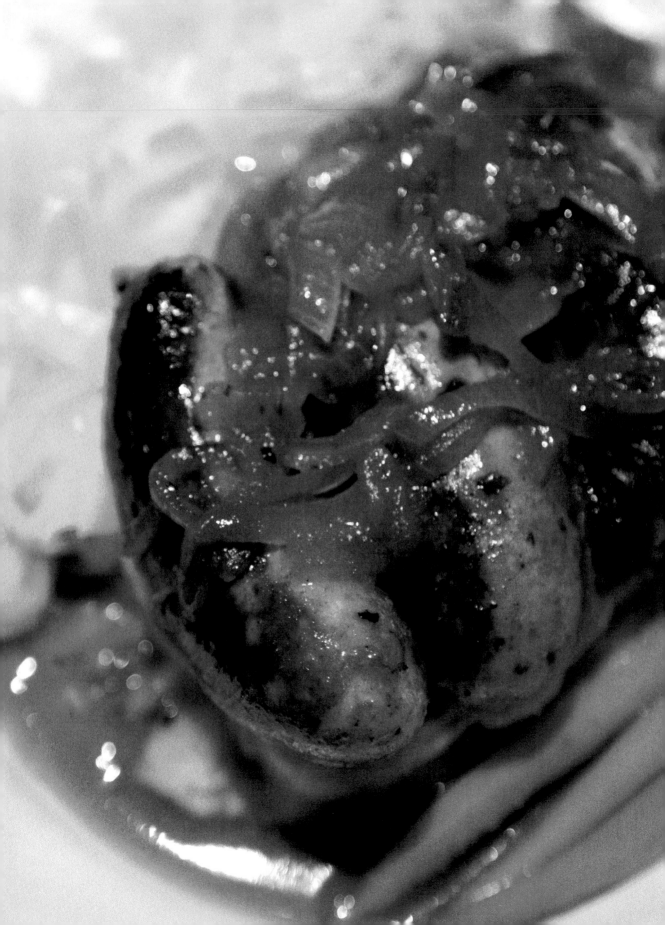

minutes, turning them now and then to make sure they don't burn. Whilst the potatoes are simmering and sausages are cooking in the oven, add your onions to the pan you fried your sausages in and cook them slowly and gently until they soften and start to turn brown. Add the wine, then bring to the boil and simmer until it reduces by half. Mix the stock cube in a bowl with the Marmite and about 275ml of boiling water from the kettle. Stir so everything dissolves and pour into the pan with your wine and onions. Add a squeeze of tomato purée or ketchup and sprinkle in the flour. Stir everything together well, then simmer for 10 minutes or so until it thickens and starts to look like a gravy. Season with a little salt and pepper.

You'll know your potatoes and parsnips are done when you can push a knife right through them. Drain them in a colander and mash with a good-sized knob of butter, plenty of salt and pepper and either the single cream if you like your mash creamy, or the low-fat milk.

Serve your parsnip mash and sausages with the onion gravy poured over the top.

Beef and thyme burgers with Roquefort cheese and rocket

Serves 4

 olive oil

 1 medium onion, peeled and chopped

 1 clove of garlic, peeled and chopped

 salt and freshly ground black pepper

 balsamic vinegar

 Worcestershire sauce

 a few sprigs of fresh thyme, leaves picked and chopped

 500g minced beef

 plain flour

 200g Roquefort cheese

Heat a splash of oil in a large frying pan and fry the onions and garlic slowly until soft. Season with salt and pepper, add a good dash of balsamic vinegar and Worcestershire sauce and stir in the chopped thyme. Fry for 30 seconds

more, then take off the heat and leave to cool down a little.

Tip the cooled mixture into a mixing bowl with the minced beef and mix everything together. Divide the mix into four equal amounts and shape into balls with your hands.

Sprinkle a plate with a little flour and place one of the balls on it. Press down with your fingers, squashing it out into a burger shape. Shape the rest of the burgers the same way and make sure they are dusted all over with flour.

Fry in a little oil, or cook on the barbeque, for 4 – 5 minutes each side. Serve them in burger buns, with a large slice of Roquefort, some dressed rocket and chunky chips (see page 85).

Mushroom, cheese and chive omelette

This is a tasty snack that's nice and easy to cook.

Serves 2

a handful of mushrooms

olive oil

a knob of butter

salt and freshly ground black pepper

4 eggs

a few fresh chives, chopped

a small handful grated Cheddar or Gruyère cheese

Wipe and trim your mushrooms, and slice them thinly. Heat a non-stick frying pan and add a splash of oil and a knob of butter. Add the mushrooms, fry gently for 2 to 3 minutes until soft, and season with salt and pepper.

Whisk up your eggs with a little more salt and pepper and pour into the pan with the mushrooms. Stir gently, then lift the edge and tilt the pan, making sure the egg mix spreads evenly. Sprinkle your chives and cheese on top and cook gently until the omelette has solidified a bit. Give the pan a little shake to check it's all binding together, then fold in half and leave on a really gentle heat for about 30 seconds before serving.

Scott's baked porcini mushroom sea bass ✳ ✳ ✳

Serves 2

    2 sea bass fillets

    salt and freshly ground black pepper

    12 new potatoes, cut in half

    olive oil

    a knob of butter

    75g porcini mushrooms, soaked in warm
      water for 20
      minutes and roughly chopped

    2 spring onions, roughly chopped

    a handful of broccoli florets

    100g French beans, trimmed

Preheat the oven to 200°C/400°F/gas mark 6.

Season the sea bass fillets with salt and pepper.

Bring a large pan of water to the boil and add the potatoes and a pinch of salt. Bring back to the boil, cook the potatoes for 5 minutes and drain. Put the potatoes into a large roasting tin, add a good glug of olive oil and mix with your hands. Roast in the preheated oven for 30 minutes, or until golden.

Heat a good glug of olive oil and a knob of butter in a frying pan. Add the sea bass fillets and pan-fry for 2 minutes each side. Once cooked, remove the fish from the pan and place on a warm plate, then add the mushrooms and spring onions to the frying pan and cook gently for 5 or so minutes until the onions are translucent and the mushrooms are warmed through.

Meanwhile, steam or boil your broccoli florets and beans for no more than 5 minutes and drain. Toss in a little olive oil and season with salt and pepper. Serve with the sea bass, mushrooms, spring onions and potatoes.

Scott's pan-fried sea bass starter ☀

You can make this into a main dish if you serve with seasonal veg and rice or potatoes.

Serves 4

> 4 x 100g pieces of sea bass
> salt and freshly ground black pepper
> plain flour
> olive oil
> fresh chives
> Lemon or lime wedges to serve

Season the sea bass with a little salt and pepper and sprinkle well with plain flour so that the pieces of fish are well dusted on each side. Preheat a non-stick frying pan and add a splash of olive oil.

Shake the excess flour off the fish and lay them skin side down in the hot pan. Fry for 2 minutes, then turn them over gently with a spatula and cook for 1 minute more. Check that the fish is cooked – if it's hot all the way through, it's done.

Lift the fish out of the pan and place on four plates. Garnish with a few fresh chives and serve with wedges of lemon or lime.

Spaghetti with spicy meatballs

This is a good winter dish. Instead of cooking a stew, which takes hours, you can have this ready in 20 minutes. I sometimes add a glass of red wine with the tomatoes. If you like it spicy, add more chilli.

Serves 4

    olive oil

    2 onions, peeled and finely chopped

    3 cloves of garlic, peeled and chopped

    a few sprigs of fresh thyme, leaves picked

    balsamic vinegar

    500ml tomato passata

    a handful of cherry tomatoes, cut in half

    1 tablespoon dried mixed herbs

    750g lean minced beef

    1 egg

    salt and freshly ground black pepper

    a few sliced mushrooms (optional)

    1 red chilli, chopped (optional)

    a splash of red wine (optional)

    a small bunch of fresh basil, leaves picked

    500g spaghetti

    grated Parmesan cheese to serve

Heat a large saucepan and add a splash of olive oil. Fry the onion and garlic for a minute or two until softened and lightly browned. Scoop half the cooked onion and garlic out into a mixing bowl and put the pan back on the heat. Add the thyme leaves and a dash of balsamic vinegar which will help tenderize the meatballs, then add the passata and tomatoes and leave to simmer gently.

Add the mixed herbs, minced beef and egg to the bowl with the cooked onion and garlic in it. Mix well and season with salt and pepper. Shape into small meatballs with your hands – if you wet your hands it'll stop the mixture sticking to them as you shape them.

Drop the meatballs into the sauce along with the mushrooms, if you're using them, and the chilli if you like things spicy, and add a splash of water or red wine to the sauce if it's a bit thick. Simmer gently with the lid on for about 15 minutes, or until the meatballs are cooked through, then stir in the basil leaves.

Cook the pasta according to the packet instructions, then drain in a colander and divide between four plates. Season the meatball sauce with a little salt and pepper and spoon over the spaghetti. Serve sprinkled with Parmesan.

Sid's easy-peasy pesto pasta ☀

Serves 2

olive oil

1 onion, peeled and sliced

2 cloves of garlic, peeled and sliced

300g chestnut mushrooms, sliced

salt and freshly ground black pepper

250g cherry tomatoes, cut in half

a squeeze of tomato purée or ketchup

4 tablespoons red pesto

4 tablespoons single cream

a small bunch of fresh basil, leaves picked

250g spaghetti

grated Parmesan cheese to serve

Heat a large frying pan and add a splash of oil. Add the onion and garlic and fry for a minute or two until softened and very lightly browned. Throw in the mushrooms and fry for a few minutes until they've softened and taken on all the flavours of the garlic and onion.

Season with salt and pepper and add the cherry tomatoes. Turn the heat down and cook, stirring now and then, until the tomatoes start to cook down into a sauce. Add a squeeze of tomato purée or ketchup, the pesto and the cream and simmer for another minute. Stir in the basil and take the pan off the heat.

Cook the pasta according to the packet instructions and drain in a colander. Stir into the sauce, season with a little salt and pepper if you need to, and serve sprinkled with Parmesan.

When I was sixteen, I got the job playing Ricky Butcher in *EastEnders*. To begin with, I was travelling up to the studios at Borehamwood in Hertfordshire, filming during the day and going back to the squat in Islington in time for tea. It might sound like a bit of an odd life, but having my brothers to go back to kept things real for me. Darren kind of held the fort and would have dinner ready for when I got back. Then I'd go and learn my lines. It was good living with my brothers again in the area where I came from, and us all cooking together. It kept some kind of normality in my life. What with *EastEnders* being such a big show, I was starting to get recognized more and more.

I'd started seeing my girlfriend, Amanda, when I was sixteen. I'd got to know her because she was the sister of one of the actors in *EastEnders*. Amanda and I were getting closer and wanted to move in together, but she lived with her dad out in Wanstead in east London, and didn't want him to be alone, so when I was seventeen I stopped squatting and moved into their house. Her father was a very, very basic cook. In fact, he didn't really cook at all. The most extravagant dish he made was Welsh rarebit. A lump of cheese and a bit of English mustard. So Amanda and I often went out to eat!

We started off just going out locally. I would have an Indian at least once a week, Italian two or three times. Because I could afford it now, I got into eating out. At the local restaurant I used to go to, John, the guy who ran it, was seriously passionate about food, and we got quite friendly. We used to go there a lot, and he would introduce us to new dishes. It was nice to have the opportunity. One day I would eat a Provençal fish dish, and the next day I would have some calves' liver or a bit of veal. They looked after us.

Coming from a background where restaurants had not really been a major part of my life, it was all an exciting new experience. It was great to be pampered and treated so well. I was starting to think about the connection between the food we were eating and the countries it came from. I still hadn't done that much travelling at this point, but these restaurants and the families who ran them began to open my eyes to the rest of the world and made me eager to experience the food in its authentic setting. For me it was all still about learning – food being very much my hobby and escape.

Pan-fried calves' liver with fresh sage

This is a posh version of liver and bacon, as calves' liver is that bit more expensive.

Serves 2

    500g potatoes

    salt and freshly ground black pepper

    400g calves' liver, cut in 1 cm thick slices

    plain flour

    butter

    a few fresh sage leaves

    2–3 tablespoons single cream or low-fat milk

Peel the potatoes, place them in a deep saucepan and cover them with water. Add a pinch of salt and bring to the boil, then turn the heat down to a simmer.

Season the slices of liver with a little salt and pepper and sprinkle well with flour so they're well coated on each side. Preheat a large, heavy frying pan and add a good knob of butter. Once the pan's hot, shake the excess flour off the slices of liver and lay them in the sizzling butter in the pan. Cook for 2 minutes, then add the sage leaves, turn over and cook for a minute more. The liver should be rosy pink in the middle, so fry it for a little longer if you prefer your liver more well done.

You'll know your potatoes are cooked when you can push a knife right through them. Drain them in a colander and mash with a good knob of butter, plenty of salt and pepper and either the single cream if you like your mash creamy, or the low-fat milk.

Serve the liver on a bed of mash, with nice green vegetables like fresh spinach, broccoli or peas.

Chicken liver salad with walnuts and Roquefort ☀

Sometimes I pan-fry the onions with the livers for a bit of extra flavour, and sometimes, like here, I use them raw for sharpness and crunch.

Serves 2 as a main or 4 as a starter

400g chicken livers, trimmed

1 small onion, peeled

1 x 200g bag of mixed salad leaves

12 cherry tomatoes, sliced in half

balsamic and olive oil dressing (see page 129)

olive oil

100g Roquefort cheese

a good handful of crushed walnuts

salt and freshly ground black pepper

Trim any white stringy bits off the chicken livers and drain them on a piece of kitchen paper. Cut the onion in half and then with a sharp knife, slice it as thinly as you can. Put the onion in a serving bowl with the salad leaves and the tomatoes. Make the balsamic dressing.

Preheat a non-stick frying pan, add a splash of oil, and fry the livers slowly for about 7–10 minutes over a medium heat. Season with salt and pepper while they're frying.

Toss the salad with the dressing, the crumbled cheese and the walnuts. Divide the salad between the plates, then drain the fat from the frying pan, lay the livers on top of the salad and serve.

At this point I was socializing more, meeting more people and making new friends. I'd always been into music and now I was getting involved in making music. Through my love of music I met a Jewish guy called Mitch, who also loved cooking. His wife was French and a great cook. This was probably my first experience of rustic French food. We used to have mussel nights once a month, if they were in season. Really it was an excuse for a piss-up, but I would help wash the mussels and watch how the sauce was made, picking up

new techniques and recipes as we went along.

As I got into my later teens, my role as Ricky Butcher developed quite a bit and I was now working most days of the week. I was earning a bit more too, so when I was nineteen or twenty I bought a flat, in Wanstead. It was a great big place, and I put in a recording studio and started running it professionally. This meant that a lot of people were coming and going all the time. One of these was a great singer called Mehmet. He was Turkish and showed me how to make great, simple Turkish food. Simplicity in cooking really appealed to me. You don't want to spend hours in the kitchen – when you come home from work, you want to be able to just bung something together. I started really taking note and wanted to learn more.

Mehmet would sometimes take us to a local Turkish restaurant, a really traditional one. I remember once he ordered a load of food. My brother Scott ate something off the platter, and then discovered it was sheep's bollocks! He liked it

even when he found out what it was – whether he'd have tried it if he'd realized beforehand, we'll never know. As usual, I'd try anything, and if I liked it, I'd try to learn how to make it. I just wanted to learn how to cook.

Moules marinières ☀

This delicious starter is one of my all-time favourites.

Serves 2

    1kg mussels

    a knob of butter

    olive oil

    3 shallots, peeled and chopped

    1 stick of celery, finely chopped

    1 clove of garlic, peeled and finely chopped

    1 glass of dry white wine

    1 small tub of double cream

    a small bunch of fresh flat-leaf parsley, washed and chopped

Wash your mussels first in plenty of cold water, pulling off any beardy bits you find on them, and throw away any that aren't tightly closed.

Heat a large saucepan or wok and add the butter and a glug of olive oil. Add the shallot, celery and garlic, and when they've fried for a couple of

minutes, add a good glass of dry white wine. Simmer for a few minutes to cook off the alcohol, then add the cream and the chopped parsley. Cook for another couple of minutes, then add the mussels.

Cover with a lid and cook for 3–5 minutes, until most of the mussels have opened. Pick out any that haven't opened and throw them away. Serve with a nice glass of Sancerre and lots of crusty bread.

Garlic prawns

Serves 2 as a starter

a big knob of butter

olive oil

4 big tiger prawns

salt and freshly ground black pepper

2 cloves of garlic, peeled and chopped

1 lemon

mixed salad to serve

Preheat your oven to 200°C/400°F/gas mark 6.

Heat a heavy ovenproof frying pan and add the butter and olive oil. When the pan is sizzling, add the prawns, season with salt and pepper and fry for 2 minutes on each side. Throw in the garlic and shake the pan so it all goes into the hot butter and oil, and place the whole pan in the preheated oven. Cook for about 5 minutes more, then serve with wedges of lemon and a little mixed salad.

Chunky chips

Always be careful when using a chip pan 'cause it's easy to forget how hot the oil can get. Just remember you've got the pan on the heat and don't let your kids or pets near the stove.

Serves 4

> 1kg sweet potatoes, peeled
>
> vegetable oil
>
> salt

With a sharp knife, trim your sweet potatoes into rectangular blocks, then into thick chips. Don't throw away your trimmings – they're great for mash or soup.

Fill a sturdy saucepan with a couple of litres of oil and place on a medium heat. Drop a piece of bread into the oil – when it starts to fry, you'll know the oil is hot enough to start cooking. Carefully drop in a few chips at a time, watching out for splashes. Make sure all the chips are under the surface of the oil – you may need to cook them in batches. Poke them around with a metal spoon or a pair of tongs to make sure they're not sticking together.

The idea is to cook them through without them going too brown. If they start to turn golden before they're soft, turn the heat down a little. When the chips have cooked for 3 or 4 minutes, lift them out of the oil with a slotted spoon, place them on a plate and let them sit for a few minutes.

Get a tray ready with a couple of layers of kitchen paper in it. When you're ready for your chips, heat the oil again and carefully drop the chips back in. This time, fry them quickly so they're brown and crisp on the outside and still fluffy and soft in the middle. Lift them out of the oil and place them on the kitchen paper to drain. Sprinkle with a good pinch of salt and shake them about in the tray to get as much oil off as possible before serving.

Tuna pasta ☼

Serves 4 to 6

olive oil

1 onion, peeled and finely chopped

1 clove of garlic, peeled and chopped

a handful of mushrooms, cleaned and sliced

1 red pepper, halved, cored and chopped

1 courgette, chopped

a few sprigs of fresh thyme, leaves picked

salt and freshly ground black pepper

1 glass of red wine

2 x 400g tins of plum tomatoes

6 cherry tomatoes, halved

1 tin of tuna, drained

a handful of black olives, stoned

a small bunch of fresh basil, leaves picked

a squeeze of tomato purée or ketchup (optional)

2 tablespoons single cream (optional)

500g fresh penne

Heat a large saucepan, add a splash of olive oil and fry the onion, garlic, mushrooms, peppers, courgettes and thyme. Season well with salt and pepper, and after about 5 minutes, when the vegetables are starting to brown, add the wine. Simmer for a minute or two to cook off the alcohol, then add the tinned tomatoes and the fresh cherry tomatoes.

Simmer for another 10 minutes or so, then stir in the tuna, the olives and half the basil leaves. If your sauce is a bit sharp, add a squeeze of tomato purée or ketchup to give your sauce a nice sweetness. A few tablespoons of single cream can work wonders too.

Cook the pasta according to the packet instructions, then drain in a colander and stir into the sauce. Season with a little salt and pepper if you need to, and serve sprinkled with the rest of the basil leaves.

Chicken fajitas

I love to make fajitas. They're quick to prepare and cook and it's great watching all your mates get stuck into the bowls of salsa and sour cream.

Serves 4

>olive oil
>
>1 red onion, peeled and chopped
>
>1 red pepper, cored and sliced
>
>1 green pepper, cored and sliced
>
>2 cloves of garlic, peeled and chopped
>
>1 fresh red chilli, chopped
>
>1 tablespoon Mexican mixed spice seasoning (or faghita seasoning)
>
>1 tablespoon tomato purée
>
>4 chicken breasts, cut into chunks
>
>salt and freshly ground black pepper
>
>sprigs of fresh coriander, chopped
>
>A few chives, chopped
>
>8 flour tortillas
>
>sour cream and tomato salsa to serve

Heat a large frying pan and add a glug of oil. Add the onion, peppers, garlic, chilli, mixed spice and tomato purée, and cook everything together for about 5 to 7 minutes until nice and soft.

Heat a second frying pan and cook the chicken in a little oil until browned all over. Season well with salt and pepper and tip into the pan with the vegetables. Cook everything together for 6 or 7 more minutes, until the chicken is cooked through.

Warm your tortillas in a low oven. Dollop the chicken mix on to them, sprinkle with the chopped coriander and chives and roll or fold them up. Serve with sour cream and tomato salsa.

I would work all week travelling between Wanstead and Hertfordshire and then I would go down to Brighton at the weekend to see my best friend, Simon. His mum would cook non-stop all week-end for us. Her speciality was a great roast, she did the best gravy. She used to take the meat out of the baking tray when it was ready and then put the tray on the hob and make up a mix with Marmite and flour. It was a long process, but it was a good, thick, stock gravy. Very tasty!

Although I had my own kitchen at home and was cooking roasts, they weren't great, so this educated me. I saw how much time Simon's mum took over all the minor details of cooking a roast. I learned that you can't just bung your potatoes in the oven, you need to parboil them and fluff them up first, to get that nice crisp coating. She would introduce other little dishes along with the roast, like butter beans in a ratatouille sauce. I think I used to drive her mad, standing around in the kitchen, watching her.

Shopping with Simon and his daughter Georgie in Brighton

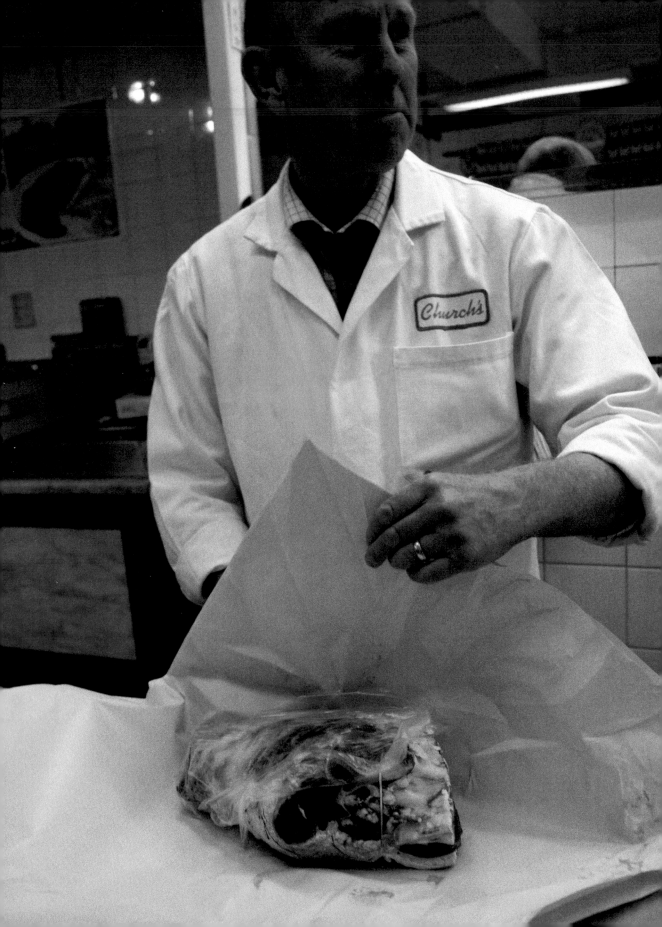

Sunday roast with gravy and fluffy roast potatoes

Sunday lunch is one of my favourite get-together meals – it's an all-day event, and everyone can get involved in preparing it, even if it's just helping to peel the veg. The trick is to use good-quality meat, marinade it to give it extra flavour, and cook it slowly, basting it often with the fat and juices from the tray as it roasts. This helps to create a nice sticky crust on the outside of the meat and keeps it really juicy. Always buy your meat for Sunday lunch on Saturday, so that you've got plenty of time for the marinade to flavour the meat.

You've also got to put a lot of love into the gravy. I cook gravy from start to finish of the roast – it's just as important as the meat. To start it off, I put half a bottle of red wine into a saucepan, perhaps with a bit of onion, and simmer it gently. Then I pour in some meat stock and add the juices that come out of the roast as it cooks. Skim off any fat that floats to the surface and save it for roasting your potatoes. You can also add some of the water you've cooked your veg in and maybe even a squeeze of orange or cranberry juice. If you put some chunky bits of onion, carrot and celery into the tray with your roast as it cooks, they'll turn brown and sticky and make all the difference to your gravy.

95

Once the meat is cooked, place it on a serving dish and let it sit for a good half an hour, covered loosely with some tinfoil. This relaxes the fibres, making it easier to carve, and gives you a chance to sort out all the things that go with it, as it's important to get things ready together and hot. Turn the oven up to crisp up your potatoes and cook your Yorkshires if you're doing them, warm up your mash in a saucepan and boil or steam your broccoli or other greens.

Don't forget to add all the resting juices – that's the juices that come out of your roast as it rests – to the gravy and, most important of all, scrape all the sticky bits off the bottom of the empty roasting tray with a little hot water and pour this into the gravy as well. This is what really makes it special. Finally, pour the gravy through a sieve so it's nice and smooth.

To make the marinade, whiz the leaves from a few sprigs of rosemary and thyme in a food processor with a few cloves of garlic and half a pack of butter. Season well with plenty of salt and pepper and even some lemon zest if you like.

For a **leg of lamb**, stab the meat all over with the tip of a sharp knife and massage the marinade in. A 2kg leg of lamb with the bone in will take 1¼ to 1½ hours in a 200°C/400°F/gas mark 6 oven, depending on how pink you like your meat. If you like it well done, an extra 15 minutes should do the trick.

For a **roast chicken**, rub the marinade all over the skin of the chicken and throw a few more sprigs of herbs, cloves of garlic and half a lemon inside it for extra flavour. A free-range medium-size chicken (about 1.5kg) will take about 1 hour 20 minutes in a 200°C/400°F/gas mark 6 oven. Cover with foil at first, and take it off 20 minutes before end of cooking so you can baste the chicken and crisp the skin up.

For a **rib of beef**, massage the marinade all over the surface of the meat and then, once rubbed in, spoon half a jar of wholegrain mustard on top, spreading a thick layer of it over the beef. This will give it a great crust as it roasts. A 2.5kg forerib of beef will take 1 hour and 40 minutes to 2 hours in a 200°C/400°F/gas mark 6 oven, depending on how pink you like your meat.

Below and overleaf: cooking with old friends, Nick Berry and family

Roast potatoes

The best fat to use for roasting your potatoes is the fat from the joint you are cooking, whether it's a chicken or a piece of beef or a leg of lamb. Collect the fat from the tray as it roasts or from the top of the gravy as you skim it, and keep it to one side until you need it for your spuds.

Serves 6

1kg potatoes, peeled

salt and freshly ground black pepper

a few tablespoons of butter

a sprig of fresh rosemary

a few cloves of garlic

Preheat your oven to 200°C/400°F/gas mark 6 if you're not doing this dish as part of a roast. Put the potatoes into a deep saucepan and cover with cold salted water. Cut the bigger ones in half so they're pretty much the same size – this means they'll cook in the same time.

Put the pan on the heat and bring to the boil, then reduce the heat and simmer for 5 to 10 minutes. Drain the potatoes well in a colander and leave them to steam for a few minutes. Toss the potatoes around a bit in the colander so the sides start to break and mush a little. This is the secret of great crispy roast potatoes.

Put the butter and a good few tablespoons of the fat from your joint into a roasting tray and heat it up in the oven. Toss the parboiled potatoes in, add the rosemary and garlic, and season well with salt and pepper. Roast in the oven for about half an hour, and then, once you've taken the meat out to rest, turn the oven up as high as it will go to crisp them up.

Carrot and swede mash

Serves 4 to 6

      1 small swede, peeled and chopped

      3 carrots, peeled and chopped

      salt and freshly ground black pepper

      a knob of butter

      2–3 tablespoons single cream or low-fat milk

Place the chopped vegetables in a deep saucepan and cover with water. Add a pinch of salt and bring to the boil, then turn the heat down to a simmer.

You'll know your veg are done when you can push a knife right through the carrots. Drain them in a colander and mash with a good-sized knob of butter, plenty of salt and pepper and the single cream, if you like your mash creamy, or low-fat milk.

Yorkshire puddings

It's important to have your oven nice and hot for this dish, and to make sure your tray is preheated in the oven before you put the batter in. The batter HAS to rest for half an hour or the puddings won't be right!

Serves 6

    2 eggs
    150g plain flour
    250ml milk
    salt and freshly ground black pepper
    vegetable oil

Crack the eggs into a mixing bowl and whisk them up. Tip in the flour and beat to a stiff paste. Pour in a little of the milk and whisk it in, then a little more and a little more. The more gradually you add your milk, the fewer lumps there will be in the batter. Season with salt and pepper, cover and leave in the fridge for at least half an hour before you use it.

Preheat the oven to 220°C/425°F/gas mark 7. Place a tablespoon of fat in each little compartment of a shallow cupcake tray and place the tray in the preheated oven. Scoop your batter mix into a jug so it's easy to pour. When the fat's smoking in the tray, open the oven door, pour a couple of tablespoons of batter into each compartment, and shut the door quickly. The batter should sizzle when it hits the oil.

Bake for 15 minutes or so, until brown and risen, and serve straight away.

Cauliflower cheese

This is a real crowd-pleaser and great served with any Sunday roast. Straight cauliflower is great, but sometimes I add a few chunks of leek to make things more interesting.

Serves 4 to 6

> 1 cauliflower, trimmed and cut into florets
>
> 50g butter
>
> 30g flour
>
> 500ml milk
>
> 1 tablespoon of grainy mustard
>
> salt and freshly ground black pepper
>
> a handful of grated mature Cheddar cheese
>
> grated Parmesan cheese (optional)

Preheat your oven to 200°C/400°F/gas mark 6.

Bring a large saucepan of salted water to the boil and drop in your cauliflower. Bring the water back to the boil and simmer the cauliflower for about 2 minutes until half cooked. Drain well.

Heat a small saucepan and put in the butter. When the butter has melted and is starting to foam, stir in the flour and keep stirring until it has formed a paste. Add the milk a splash at a time, stirring it well into the paste before adding more. The more slowly you do this, the smoother your sauce will be. When you've added all the milk and the sauce has come to the boil, take off the heat and add the mustard, a few pinches of salt and pepper and the Cheddar.

Tip the drained cauliflower into a baking dish and pour the cheese sauce over the top. Sprinkle with the Parmesan if you're using it, and bake in the preheated oven for about half an hour, until hot through and crispy brown on top.

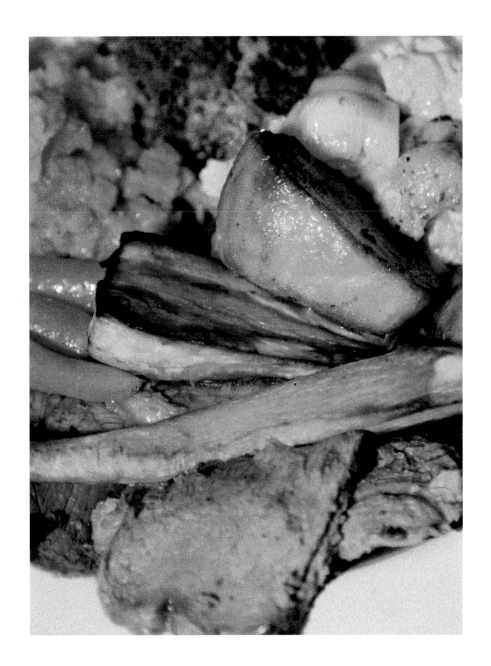

Rachel's butternut squash soup

Nick's wife, Rachel, gave me the recipe for this delicious soup. I love it really spicy, but do adjust the amount of chilli powder you use according to your taste.

Serves 4

    1 whole large butternut squash

    1 carrot

    1 stick of celery

    a knob of butter

    olive oil

    1 large onion, peeled and chopped

    1 teaspoon ground cumin

    ½ teaspoon chilli powder or more if you like it very hot

    1 litre chicken stock (this can be substituted for vegetable stock)

    salt and freshly ground black pepper

    2–3 tablespoons double cream

    chopped fresh coriander to garnish

Peel the squash with a potato peeler and cut it in half lengthways. Scoop out the seeds with a spoon and throw them away, then chop the squash up into chunks. Peel the carrot and chop into chunks and clean and chop the stick of celery.

Heat a large deep saucepan and add a knob of butter and splash of olive oil. Fry the squash with the onion, the carrot and the celery gently over a low heat until everything's

starting to soften – about 10–15 minutes. Add the cumin, chilli powder and stock, and bring to the boil.

Simmer gently for 15–20 minutes until the squash is soft, then take off the heat and blitz with a stick blender. Put the soup back on the heat and season with salt and pepper. Stir in the cream, and serve with the fresh coriander leaves sprinkled over the top.

Rachel preparing her soup

During this time I had the chance to go to Florida, because Simon's family had a holiday home there. That was where I learned to make gazpacho. I like the simplicity of seeing cucumber, peppers, garlic, tomatoes, just put in a blender and mixed up with a bit of oil and Tabasco and lemon juice. It looked healthy and it tasted good, with that bit of spice. It was a completely new taste for me.

Simon's mum was always cooking. She really liked it, and got great pleasure out of starting from nothing, creating a tasty meal and watching people enjoy what she'd made. It was a comforting thing in a way, taking me back to childhood memories growing up with my brothers. Food can be an escape from things; it's kind of reassuring to be around food and people who like it.

I used to try to do my bit to return the generosity of Simon's family by shopping and cooking a meal for them now and then. I would do a nice barbie, basic simple food. I enjoyed going to the supermarkets too, especially abroad, seeing all the different things that people eat. It helps you understand a country a bit more if you look at what they have in their supermarkets. And it can give you inspiration.

I can't understand why when people go away abroad they head straight for the English section at the supermarket. Have a bit of creativity and broaden your horizons!

By the age of about twenty-one I was experiencing so much at home, in my personal life, making friends through food and doing all this cooking, that I realized the catering on set at that time was a bit disappointing. The only healthy thing at the studio was jacket potato with cottage cheese and salad.

Gazpacho

Serves 4

- 1 red pepper
- 1 green pepper
- juice of 1 lime
- $\frac{1}{2}$ a cucumber
- 1 red or white onion, peeled
- 1 clove of garlic, peeled
- 2 tablespoons good olive oil
- 1 tablespoon white wine vinegar
- a dash of Tabasco sauce
- 1 x 400g tin of plum tomatoes
- salt and freshly ground black pepper

Cut the peppers in half and pull out the core and seeds with your fingers. Chop the pepper flesh roughly and put the pieces into a blender along with all the other ingredients. Whiz until smooth, then pour into a container and add a little salt and pepper. Cover the soup and put into the fridge for an hour, or even longer, for the flavours to develop.

Taste before serving and add a little more salt and pepper, and more Tabasco if you want the gazpacho to have more of a kick to it.

Sid's chicken Caesar salad

Serves 2

    1 x 200g jar of mayonnaise

    100g Parmesan cheese, grated, plus more for serving

    4 salted anchovy fillets, chopped

    Tabasco sauce

    Worcestershire sauce

    lemon juice

    salt and freshly ground black pepper

    2 slices of stale bread, ripped into pieces

    1 small clove of garlic, peeled and chopped

    2 chicken breasts, skin off

    1/2 an iceberg or a whole cos or romaine lettuce, washed and torn

    a couple of ripe tomatoes, chopped

    1 small red onion, peeled and finely sliced

Scoop the mayonnaise into a mixing bowl and add the Parmesan, anchovies, a dash of Worcester and Tabasco, a squeeze of lemon juice and a good pinch of salt and pepper.

Heat a frying pan and add a splash of oil, the torn-up bread and the garlic. Fry gently until the bread turns golden and crisp, then take off the heat and keep warm.

Slice the chicken into small strips and season all over with salt and pepper. Heat a griddle pan, add a drizzle of oil and griddle the chicken for about 4 minutes on each side.

Put the lettuce into the serving bowl first, then add the tomatoes and onion, then the cooked chicken. Pour the dressing over the top and mix everything together. Divide between two plates, sprinkle with a little more Parmesan and the warm croutons and serve.

One time when I was in Florida with my girlfriend, a Jamaican friend of mine was back in Kingston and he invited me over. I jumped on a flight and went to traditional, hardcore Jamaica. The first place I went to was Kingston, and I remember eating the proper jerk chicken and the patties. While I was there I went to a Jamaican wedding and ate goat. The Jamaicans love goat. At weddings, the traditional dish is called Mannish Water, which is basically the intestines of the goat. That wasn't the greatest experience. Intestines were a bridge too far – too much skin! The actual broth tasted nice, but it's something I would taste once but not again, unless I was at a Jamaican wedding of course.

It was there that I learned to do my little Jamaican breakfast. You fry up onions and peppers, just to add a bit more taste to some baked beans. You put the beans in, and to spice it up, you put in a little bit of hot sauce, and then fry up some plantain. And they wouldn't have sausages; they'd have chicken frankfurters, because they don't eat pork, being Rastafarians. Sandra, my agent, who's Jamaican, showed me how to cook with plantain, which is very tasty. Try it, it's a lovely little breakfast.

Even in London, round the corner from her office, Sandra would take me to a little yard shop. They would do lovely stews, and ackee and swordfish. Really nice, tasty dishes, with rice and a bit of coleslaw. I loved that – it was the spice again!

Sandra's first husband is from Barbados, and that was one of the reasons I was interested in going there. The first time I went I got into scuba-diving. The guy I was diving with was Bajan. I made friends with him and his wife and they took me to the local restaurants, good traditional Bajan places. I loved the markets, where you'd get tasty, fresh produce. The fish was lovely in Barbados, straight off the boats. And it was flying fish that really stuck with me. It was the first time I had eaten it. It's quite a clean little white fish – it was just the way they cooked it, in a really light batter. As I hope you'll discover from trying some of the recipes in this book, good ingredients, simply prepared can produce big flavour results.

Sandra's mum's West Indian salmon

I love this dish that Sandra makes. The salmon barely needs any cooking at all and comes out soft, juicy and tasty!

Serves 4

>4 pieces of fresh salmon
>
>juice of 1 lemon
>
>4fl oz water
>
>2 large carrots, peeled and sliced like chips
>
>2 onions, diced
>
>a good knob of butter
>
>2 teaspoons mixed herbs
>
>2 cloves of garlic, crushed
>
>salt and freshly ground black pepper

Put the salmon into a bowl and add the lemon juice and water. Leave to stand for 10–15 minutes.

Lay the sliced carrots on the bottom of a large saucepan and place the salmon fillets on top. Lay the diced onion on top of the salmon and sprinkle over a pinch of salt, some freshly ground black pepper, the mixed herbs and the butter. Cover with the pan lid, gently bring the pan to a simmer and cook for 10 minutes.

Serve with a selection of vegetables, which could include steamed cabbage, steamed broccoli, boiled potatoes or steamed cauliflower.

Jamaican spicy snapper

Serves 4

  2 whole red snappers about 800g each

  2 tablespoons fish seasoning

  2 teaspoons smoked paprika

  salt and freshly ground black pepper

  olive oil

  2 cloves of garlic, peeled and chopped

  3 peppers (yellow, orange and red), cored and sliced

  2 x 400g tins of tomatoes

  1 lemon, zested and juiced

  a few sprigs of fresh flat-leaf parsley, chopped

For the rice

  1 cup of rice

  2 cups of water

  1/2 a vegetable stock cube

When you buy your snappers, make sure they're nice and fresh and get the fishmonger to scale them, gut them and cut the gills out. When you get them home, wash them inside and out and pat them dry with kitchen paper.

Lay the fish on a chopping board. With a sharp knife, slash them three times on each side. Mix the fish seasoning with the paprika and a few pinches of salt and sprinkle over the fish. Drizzle with a little oil and rub the seasoning all over the fish, making sure it goes right into the slashes. Put the fish to one side to marinate for about half an hour.

Heat a large saucepan or sturdy baking tray big enough to hold both fish at once but don't put the fish in yet. Pour in a splash of oil, add the garlic and peppers and cook gently for about 10 minutes, until the peppers are soft and sweet. Add the tomatoes and simmer for another 15 minutes, seasoning with a little salt and pepper.

Now lay the fish side by side in the pan on top of the peppers and tomatoes, and squeeze the lemon juice over the top. Cover with a lid or a piece of foil and simmer over a low heat for about 30 minutes. Put the rice and the water into a saucepan with the stock cube and bring to the boil without stirring. Turn the heat down, cover with a lid and leave to simmer for about 15 minutes.

Check the fish is hot through – if it is, it's cooked. By now the rice should have absorbed all the water and be nice and fluffy. Spoon it on to four plates, drizzle with some olive oil and sprinkle with a little lemon zest and chopped parsley. Serve the snapper in the saucepan at the table so that everyone can help themselves.

3

a taste of the country

When I was twenty-five, I moved from London to Cambridge, to a little village called Alconbury. I'd been living hard for a while – and not just with working on *EastEnders*. I'd been partying in a big way, was out most nights and I'd got into one or two dodgy situations. It was all starting to get a bit out of control, so moving out of London seemed like a really good way of calming down and getting my head together.

Being in the country was a totally new experience. There was a great butcher's shop in the village that sold all kinds of meat. Because it was the countryside, local people would go hunting; I wasn't at all into that, but I was intrigued by the new tastes this offered. It was the first time I had tried venison, for example. Because it was such a great shop I would go every Saturday and get my week's worth of meat – I soon got to know the butcher.

In the house where I lived, I had a lovely kitchen with an Aga. The Aga took a while to get used to, but it made me want to cook even more. It's almost easier to cook with than a normal stove because it's there, ready, with a warm oven and a hot hob. That Aga was on twenty-four hours a day. At first it was hard to balance that in-between heat. I burnt my hands almost every day, just trying to get used to it. But once I'd mastered it, I got great results (and a nice warm house).

One of the things about an Aga that is better than a conventional oven is the slow cooking. It encouraged me to try a different kind of cooking. It made me want to bake more stuff and try different and more elaborate dishes, like the kleftiko recipe you'll find in this book. Behind the house I had a few acres. Because I was busy working on *EastEnders* at this point, I didn't have a lot of time to grow anything, but I did grow my own herbs and my kind neighbour took care of my greenhouses.

Kleftiko

Serves 4

    8 fat neck of lamb chops

    3 cloves of garlic, peeled and sliced

    3 sprigs of fresh rosemary

    1 litre lamb stock

    salt and freshly ground black pepper

    1 large onion

    4 carrots

    5 potatoes

Preheat your oven to 150°C/300°F/gas mark 3.

Lay the lamb chops in a deep baking tray and spread the sliced garlic over them. Strip the rosemary leaves off the stalks and add them to the tray with the lamb stock. Season with a little salt and pepper, cover tightly with foil and place in the preheated oven for an hour.

Meanwhile peel your onion and carrots and cut them into chunks. Peel your potatoes, leaving the small ones whole and cutting the bigger ones in half. When the lamb chops have had their hour, take the tray out of the oven, add the chopped veg and cover the tray with the foil again. Bake for a further hour and a half to 2 hours before serving.

Green leaf salad

This is a really simple salad that I especially love to make with curly green French lettuce – but any other variety of lettuce will do instead. Just make sure it's nice and fresh and crisp.

Serves 4

> a nice green lettuce
>
> French dressing (see page 129)
>
> salt and freshly ground black pepper

Pull any battered or broken leaves off the outside of the lettuce and snap the rest of the leaves off into a basinful of cold water. Wash the lettuce gently with your hands and lift out into a colander. Drain well and spin dry in a salad spinner.

Toss the lettuce in a large bowl with the dressing and a little salt and pepper, and serve.

Salad Dressing

To make any of these dressings, all you have to do is measure out the ingredients and whisk them together in a small bowl. Taste to make sure you have the right balance of sharpness, and add a little more oil, lemon or lime juice, or vinegar if you need to. Season with a little salt and freshly ground black pepper before serving. These dressings should dress enough salad for 4 people.

Mediterranean dressing

100ml extra virgin olive oil
1 tablespoon balsamic vinegar
a squeeze of lemon juice

French dressing

1 small clove of garlic, peeled
and grated
100ml extra virgin olive oil
1 tablespoon white wine
vinegar
a squeeze of lemon juice
½ a teaspoon Dijon mustard

Chilli dressing

1 small clove of garlic, peeled
and grated
a small piece of root ginger,
grated
4 tablespoons Thai fish sauce
4 tablespoons fresh lime juice
a small fresh red chilli, finely
chopped
a pinch of sugar
a sprig of fresh mint, chopped
a sprig of fresh coriander,
chopped

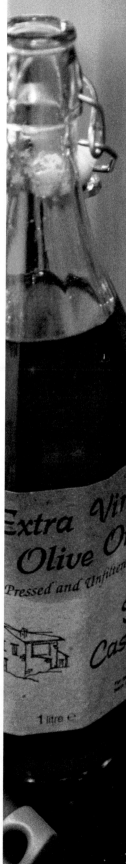

Sid's spicy coleslaw ☀

If you make this the day before, the flavours will get even better overnight in the fridge.

Serves 4

       4–5 tablespoons mayonnaise

       2 good squirts of salad cream

       a couple of good dashes of Tabasco

       a small pinch of chilli flakes

       salt and freshly ground black pepper

       ½ a white cabbage

       2 good-sized carrots, peeled

       1 medium onion, peeled

Mix the mayonnaise in a big salad bowl with the salad cream, Tabasco, chilli flakes and a good pinch of salt and pepper.

Shred the cabbage and onion finely with a sharp knife and scrape into the bowl on top of the dressing. Grate the carrots into the bowl and toss everything together. Leave for a few minutes for all the flavours to mix, then taste and add a little more salt and pepper or another squeeze of salad cream if you need to.

At that point in my life I was starting to get into eating seasonally. I was spending a lot of time with my mate Jamie Wood, son of Ronnie and Jo, and I'd often be round at their house for dinner. Jo's a great cook and 100 per cent committed to eating seasonally and organic. She's been growing her own veg in their garden in Richmond, long before it was the trendy thing to do. She really inspired me and got me into that whole way of buying and eating food. Living in the country, I could see for myself how the food I loved was produced and it got me thinking about the connection between growing and produce, and eating with the seasons.

I'd loved food for years, but apart from my travels I'd always lived in London, and now, living bang in the middle of a farming community, I was learning a lot more. You could get everything you needed – more or less – in the village farm shop and at the butcher's. The farm shop was full of seasonal fruit and veg, and the butcher would recommend different cuts of meat. The butcher's had been there for over twenty years and they were passionate about their meat, making the best sausages and pâtés for miles around. During the five years I lived there they expanded by opening up a deli counter selling local cheese and their own pies. This is a trend that's happening more and more now, but it was rare in the mid-nineties.

My neighbours would also supply me with fruit and veg from their gardens and greenhouses, so I was developing my cooking according to what was available round about. Because it was a big house and I had a large dining table, I started to have dinner parties. People would come up and visit at weekends and I'd cook meals for us all. Having all that space and in such great surroundings made me want to stay at home. And the more time I spent at home, the more I experimented in the kitchen, and the more my confidence in cooking grew. When I'd lived in London, socializing had been all about going out to restaurants, pubs and clubbing, now suddenly for the first time I had a proper home and a kitchen, and that became the centre of my social life.

I was inundated with visitors. Scott and Darren would come for the weekend and Scott would spend a fortune in the butcher's. So there we were, us three cooking with each other again. We'd go out and stock up in the farm shop and at the butcher's, and we'd spend the weekend messing about in the kitchen, experimenting with different dishes.

Although I did a lot of the cooking myself, friends like Mehmet and Mitch were also into food, so we had something in common and we'd really buzz off each other. I was a lot younger than them and was eager to learn from them. I think the passion for food spread among all my mates. Simon often came up to Cambridge to visit, and because he loves cooking as well, we'd share the work between us. Food unites people. It's a labour of love and a release from the pressures of work.

Nachos with melted cheese, jalapeños and sour cream

I love this delicious snack; it's easy to make and great to eat with your mates in front of the TV or when you're hungry after a night out at the pub.

a bowlful of my special chopped tomato relish (see page 206)

170g tortilla chips

2 fresh jalapeño chillies, diced

100g Cheddar cheese, grated

100g Monterey Jack cheese, grated

285ml sour cream, to serve

Preheat the oven to 200°C/400°F/gas mark 6.

Spread a layer of relish in the base of a large shallow ovenproof dish and sprinkle with enough tortilla chips to cover it completely. Scatter over the freshly chopped jalapeños and the Cheddar and Monterey Jack cheese, and place in the oven for about 15 minutes, or until the cheese has melted.

Remove from the oven and serve with the sour cream.

Spicy caramel nuts

These nuts are perfect at Christmas time.

300g pecan nuts or mixed nuts

3 tablespoons melted butter

¼ cup brown sugar

1 teaspoon salt

½ teaspoon chilli powder

½ teaspoon ground allspice

½ teaspoon ground cumin

1 ¾ teaspoons cayenne pepper

Preheat the oven to 200°C/400°F/gas mark 6.

Place the nuts in the oven on a low shelf for 15 minutes or until warmed through.

Meanwhile, put the butter, sugar, salt, chilli powder, allspice, cumin and cayenne pepper into a bowl and mix well with a wooden spoon. After 15 minutes, remove the nuts from the oven, pour the spice mix over them and give the tray a good shake to mix it all in.

Place the nuts back in the oven and toast for a further 10 minutes.

Sid's special garlic bread

This is great as a snack or serve it as a starter when your friends come round for dinner.

Serves 4

> 100g butter
>
> 4 cloves of garlic, peeled and finely chopped
>
> extra virgin olive oil
>
> 2 small ciabatta loaves
>
> a small bunch of fresh flat-leaf parsley, washed and drained

Preheat your oven to 220°C/425°F/gas mark 7.

Melt the butter in a small saucepan and when it starts to sizzle, add the chopped garlic and a good glug of olive oil. Take off the heat and put to one side.

Slice your loaves horizontally into two pieces as if you were making a sandwich. Pour the garlic butter all over the cut sides of the slices and spread out with a knife. Chop the parsley finely and sprinkle it all over the butter.

Place the pieces of bread butter side up on a baking tray in the preheated oven for 7–10 minutes, until nicely toasted, then drizzle with a little more olive oil and serve.

Mini skins with Roquefort and rocket ✳ ✳

This delicious starter is my take on the classic potato skins.

Serves 4 to 6

> 500g new potatoes, scrubbed
>
> salt and freshly ground black pepper
>
> 100g Roquefort cheese
>
> a handful of rocket leaves, finely chopped

Preheat your oven to 200°C/400°F/gas mark 6.

Place your potatoes in a deep saucepan and cover with cold salted water. Turn on the heat and bring to the boil. Simmer gently for about 10 to 15 minutes – you'll know the potatoes are cooked when you can just put a knife through them. Try not to overcook them, as you'll need them to hold their shape when they come out of the water. Drain in a colander and allow to cool.

When the potatoes are cool enough to handle, cut them in half lengthways and scoop out most of the insides with a teaspoon. Make sure you leave a bit of potato round the edge to hold the sides up. Put all the scooped-out potato into a bowl, add the Roquefort and a little black pepper and mash with the back of a spoon until smooth.

Sprinkle some rocket into each potato shell, top with a teaspoon of cheesy potato filling and press down. Add more rocket and filling until the potatoes are nice and full, then place them on a baking tray and put into the preheated oven. Bake for about 20 minutes, until the cheese has melted and browned on top, and the potatoes are warmed through. Serve sprinkled with any chopped rocket you have left over.

Lamb and mint burgers

Serves 4

olive oil

1 medium onion, peeled and chopped

1 clove of garlic, peeled and chopped

salt and freshly ground black pepper

balsamic vinegar

Worcestershire sauce

a few sprigs of fresh mint, leaves picked and chopped

500g minced lamb

plain flour

Heat a splash of oil in a large frying pan and fry the onions and garlic slowly until soft. Season with salt and pepper, add a good dash of balsamic vinegar and Worcestershire sauce and stir in the chopped mint. Fry for 30 seconds more, then take off the heat and leave to cool down a little.

Tip the cooled mixture into a mixing bowl with the minced lamb and mix everything together. Divide the mixture into four equal amounts and shape into balls with your hands.

Sprinkle a plate with a little flour and place one of the balls on it. Press down with your fingers, squashing it out into a burger shape. Shape the rest of the burgers the same way and make sure they are dusted all over with flour.

Fry the burgers in a little oil, or cook on the barbecue, for 4 to 5 minutes each side. Serve them in burger buns, with a little dressed rocket and chunky chips (see page 85).

I'd been into West Indian music and culture for some time, and learning more and more about the food through travel and friends. Sandra, and her then husband had taught me some dishes and Sand would come up to visit me in Cambridge and stay the weekend. Because I've known her since just after my mum died, she's like a mother figure to me. Sandra loved cooking for us, and that opened my mind to other dishes. Her speciality was slow cooking, marinating all the meat in a Bajan seasoning. She would soak it all, let it marinate, put it in a cooking bag, then cook it nice and slowly in the Aga. The Aga was great for slow roasting. You could leave meat for three or four hours, to tenderize. Lovely. We'd eat it with rice, or sometimes Sandra would do extra crispy roast potatoes, and make up a gravy or sauce from the juices of the meat.

This was different from the conventional gravy – it was more raw, just using the juices or adding a bit of pepper sauce. It didn't really need a hot sauce, but I do like my spice!

Another friend who used to come up and visit was the guy who did the rap bit in one of my records. His name was Chucky Star. He's Jamaican and would cook up mean Jamaican dishes. He loves his food and he knew that I liked cooking, so I would ask him to come and show me some new stuff. He taught me how to cook a really simple spicy West Indian snapper. It was great to add another spicy kind of cooking to my repertoire.

Sandra's Jamaican seasoning

Sandra's Jamaican seasoning goes well with any meat. Because it's nice with anything, she always makes a big batch and stores it in plastic bottles in the freezer for up to a year. The measurements below are based on one of Sandra's big batches so please do halve the amounts if you'd like to start out with a little less! Use dried herbs if you cannot find fresh ones.

6 bunches of spring onions, topped and tailed and finely chopped

3 large onions, diced

1 red pepper, chopped

1 green pepper, chopped

1 yellow pepper, chopped

1 clove of garlic, chopped

1 stick of celery, chopped

a bunch of fresh thyme, leaves roughly chopped

a bunch of fresh parsley, leaves roughly chopped

a bunch of fresh basil, leaves roughly chopped

a bunch of fresh marjoram

a bunch of fresh oregano

a bunch of fresh rosemary, leaves roughly chopped

1 tablespoon jerk seasoning

1 tablespoon dried paprika

2 teaspoons ground pimento

a pinch of freshly ground black pepper

4fl oz white wine vinegar (or enough to make the mixture moist, but not runny)

Put all the chopped herbs into a blender with the spring onions, onions, peppers, garlic and celery and whiz until smooth. Once blended, transfer to a big bowl and add the spices and pepper to taste. Finally, add the white wine vinegar to bind the ingredients and taste to see if you need to add any more spice. If it's not hot enough, add a bit more pimento.

Place in a sealed plastic container and store in the freezer if you're not going to use it straight away.

Jamaican jerk chicken

This chicken is delicious barbecued, but you can also fry it or even roast it in the oven.

Serves 4

a selection of chicken pieces – 4 thighs and 4 legs

the juice of 2 lemons

a pinch of salt

8fl oz water

Sandra's Jamaican seasoning (see page 139)

2 teaspoons paprika

2 teaspoons curry powder

2 teaspoons jerk seasoning

Put the lemon juice, salt and water into a large bowl and add the chicken pieces. Stir, then leave to marinade for 10-15 minutes, or longer if desired.

Take the chicken out of the bowl and, with the smooth side of the thigh or leg on the chopping board, cut a slit on both sides of the bone and stuff with Sandra's Jamaican seasoning.

Put the paprika, curry powder and jerk seasoning into a separate bowl and mix well. Turn the chicken in the bowl one piece at a time, using your hands to

make sure all surfaces are covered with the seasoning. Put the chicken on a dish, cover, and place in the fridge to marinate. Leave for 24 hours before cooking to really let the flavours develop.

If you're going to cook the chicken pieces on the barbecue, partially cook them in the oven first, for 30 minutes at 150°C. Remove from the oven and cook on the barbecue for a further 15–20 minutes, turning regularly. Remove once the chicken has an even colour. Serve with rice and peas and plantain.

Sandra's Jamaican pork ☼

Serves 4

4 large pork chops

4fl oz Sandra's Jamaican seasoning

1 teaspoon paprika

1 teaspoon tamarind

2 cloves of garlic, peeled and crushed

freshly ground black pepper

1 teaspoon curry powder (optional)

a pinch of salt

Place the pork chops in an ovenproof dish and pour over the Jamaican seasoning. Add the paprika, tamarind, garlic and curry powder. Sprinkle with salt and pepper. Place the dish in the fridge and leave the meat to marinade overnight.

Preheat the oven to 150°C/300°F/gas mark 2. Once the flavours have had plenty of time to infuse, place the meat in its dish in the preheated oven – the juices from the meat will quickly emerge and will keep the meat nice and moist. Cook for 1 hour 15 minutes, or until the chops are golden brown.

Serve with roast potatoes (see page 100) and steamed broccoli, or any vegetable of your choice.

Sandra's rice and peas ☀ ☀

This classic Jamaican side is pretty versatile, as you can use any bean you like. There's kidney beans, crab eye peas, gunga peas … the choice is yours. Sandra recommends kidney beans, which is what we've based this recipe on. When you measure the rice and water, make sure you use the same size cup – it's a volume measurement.

Serves 4

100g kidney beans, tinned or dried (soaked overnight)

⅓ packet of coconut cream

1½ cups of rice

3 cups water

a pinch of salt

freshly ground black pepper

a handful of fresh thyme

1 onion

a knob of butter

If you decide to use dried kidney beans, soak them in water overnight. After soaking, drain the beans, place them in a saucepan and cover them with cold water, roughly 2 inches. Add the creamed coconut to the pan and bring the water to the boil. Once boiled, turn the heat down to a simmer and cook for 1 hour. Drain the beans, but keep the water to one side, and place the cooked beans back in the pan.

If you're using tinned beans, drain them and put them into a saucepan with 1 cup of water and the creamed coconut. Bring the water to the boil, then turn down to a simmer and cook for 10–15 minutes. Drain and put back into the pan.

Put the rice in a colander and give it a good rinse under the cold tap. Add the rice to the pan with the beans and pour over the leftover water so that the rice and beans are completely covered. Add a touch of salt and pepper, the thyme and the chopped onion and bring the water to the boil. Turn the heat right down and simmer until the rice is cooked. The rice should absorb all the waer so there's no need to drain. Serve.

Plantain

Plantain should be bought a few days before you are going to use it. You can tell a good one by the colour of the skin – yellow, like a fresh banana, with some small brown marks on the skin. You know that it is ready to eat when there is a slight soft feel when you hold it. Think of a ripe banana ready to eat but not covered in freckles.

Serves 6

2 plantains, skinned and cut into 18 even pieces

olive oil

salt and freshly ground black pepper

Heat a splash of olive oil in a frying pan and pile in the peeled and diced plantain. Cook on a low heat until the pieces are golden brown, roughly 3–5 minutes each side.

Around the mid-nineties I started to travel more widely abroad. Going to Thailand was a big eye-opener. I had never seen anything like it before. I'd heard about Thailand through friends and watching documentaries, and of course I'd eaten Thai food in England, but being there allowed me to try the proper traditional stuff – like sea bass steamed in chilli and nam jim (a mixture of garlic, chillies and fish sauce). I first went there with Scott and we stayed in a hotel in Koh Samui. Koh Samui is quite commercial now, but it was a relatively small town at that point. They still have great restaurants, although there's far more places for tourists now. Ten years ago it was easier to go and experience the real Thailand, and that's what we did, meeting as many Thai people as we could along the way. We went to really basic restaurants, the same places the locals went to, and I tried to taste as much different food as I could. The atmosphere was great – you'd get the smells and sounds of the cooking as you walked along the road. The restaurants were outdoors on the street and they would literally cook in front of you, so you knew what you were getting. I developed a great love of Thailand and made many friends there.

Some years later, I started spending a lot more time in Thailand, around two or three months a year. I just loved the way of life there, and obviously the food was a big part of that. I remember this great restaurant in Bangkok which must had at least 2,000 seats spread over four floors. Its speciality was fish, and it was chocker with tanks where you'd go and pick whatever you wanted. It was good traditional Thai food. I would go there with Thai people I'd got friendly with, and they'd know what to order.

What kept taking me back there was obviously the great weather but also the chance to detox. I got into detoxing in a big way. The first time I did it I

was a bit apprehensive, because basically you don't eat for a week, you just drink detox juices. It was a bit like an MOT. It made me think afterwards about the kind of food I was eating too. It gave me a good insight into healthier cooking and healthier living. It does make you realize that you need to be careful about what you eat. It's a cliché, but it's true, you are what you eat. Before I started detoxing I'd maybe pig out now and then, but detoxing made me more aware of the effects of pigging out so I started to do it less.

It's a cheaper way of living out there. You can eat great food for very little money: £5 to £10 a day and you are eating like a king. I wanted to learn a bit more about Thai food as well, so I went and did a Thai cooking course and learned the basics. You quickly learn that most Thai food is cooked with the same staple ingredients, but they play about with them according to the dish. You've got your ginger, galangal, coriander, garlic, lemongrass, coconut milk and chillies, obviously lots of chillies – six or seven ingredients, altered and cooked in different ways. One thing I didn't really get into was learning about Thai pastes. I can make pastes, but even Thai people would tell you it is just as good to buy them ready-made. So people should not be frightened of cooking Thai stuff. As soon as they understand the ingredients, it's easy. The first dish I did was tom yum soup, which is made of tom yum paste, hot water, lemongrass, coriander, galangal and onions if you want to add a little bit of veg – you can create it how you wish. You just mix your paste, your hot water, your broth and your vegetables.

I also travelled around Thailand and experienced a lot of restaurants along the way. I did a few of the islands, which were lovely. I remember one hotel I'd stay in when I was in Koh Samui which did a really nice curried crab. Really simple, little crabs in curry powder, a bit of coconut milk, a spring onion and ginger. I got very friendly with the people who owned the hotel. They knew I was passionate about food and I would often sit down and eat with them as a family. There were two or three generations of family sitting down, from kids to grandparents. About fifty people in total. There would be lots of food in the middle of the table, with people dipping in and helping themselves. In general, Thai people are very small and slim so I was amazed by how much food they put away! While I was in Thailand, Koh Samui was where I mostly stayed, but I travelled around, to Koh Tao, Koh Pha Ngan, Koh Phi Phi, Koh Samet, and other little islands I can't remember the names of.

Koh Phi Phi is the one destroyed by the tsunami. I was there around the time of the tsunami and just after. Obviously it had affected the people and the cities as well. But people just get on with it and keep the tourism going. As a result, Samui got a bit more over-populated because the surrounding islands were hit quite hard.

This experience of going out and detoxing in Thailand was to make me all the better prepared for being on *I'm A Celebrity Get Me Out Of Here* a couple of years later. More so than the other celebrities, because I shouldn't think any of them had experienced such an enforced lack of food before. I don't know how much the viewers are aware that the contestants do really kind of get starved out there. Because I was soon to find out that I was one of the few that could cook, I became quite popular in my attempts to turn those bloody awful tiny rations of beans and rice into something edible.

151

Thai spicy salmon with pak choi and chilli noodles

Serves 2

For the fish

vegetable oil

2 pieces of salmon fillet

2 large spring onions

1 small red chilli, finely chopped

a 5cm piece of freshly grated ginger

2 small cloves of garlic, peeled and chopped

2 tablespoons soy sauce

a small bunch of fresh coriander, leaves picked

For the pak choi

sesame oil

2 heads of pak choi

50ml chicken stock or freshly boiled water

oyster sauce

For the chilli noodles

sesame oil

2 cloves of garlic, peeled and chopped

½ a fresh red chilli, finely chopped

200g ready-cooked egg noodles

Preheat your oven to 200°C/400°F/gas mark 6. Tear two sheets of foil a little bigger than a double page of this book. Rub the middle of each piece with a little vegetable oil and place the fish on top. Slice the spring onions thinly on the diagonal into long strips. Lay the spring onions on top of each fish and sprinkle over the chilli, ginger and garlic. Spoon 1 tablespoon of soy sauce on top and wrap each piece of fish up in foil, leaving a little space inside each parcel for the fish to steam. Place the parcels on a baking tray and cook in the preheated oven for 10–15 minutes.

Heat a saucepan and add a splash of sesame oil. Once the oil is heated add the pak choi and fry for a minute on each side. Pour in the stock or water and simmer until the water has reduced to nothing and the pak choi is cooked through. Pour a little oyster sauce over the top, cook for 30 seconds or so to warm up the sauce, then take off the heat.

To cook the chilli noodles, heat a non-stick frying pan and add a splash of sesame oil, the garlic and the chilli. Once sizzling, add the noodles and a little water. Stir fry for a few minutes, until the noodles are warmed through and the water has all been absorbed.

Carefully remove the tray from the oven and unwrap the fish. Check that it's hot all the way through – if it is, it's cooked. Serve the fish with the fresh coriander leaves, pak choi and chilli noodles.

Tom yum soup with prawns

Serves 2

a tablespoon tom yum paste

500ml chicken stock

a stick of lemon grass

4 cherry tomatoes, sliced

8 raw tiger prawns, peeled

4 spring onions, trimmed and finely sliced

a small bunch of fresh coriander, leaves picked

a small bunch of fresh basil, leaves picked

salt and freshly ground black pepper

Put the tom yum paste into a deep saucepan with the stock and place on the heat. Bash the lemon grass with the bottom of a saucepan until it's crushed and flattened, and it smells all lemony. Pop the lemon grass into the pot, bring to the boil and simmer for about 15 minutes.

Add the tomatoes and the prawns and bring back to the boil. Cook for 3 or 4 minutes, then take off the heat, season with salt and pepper, and ladle into the soup bowls making sure the prawns are evenly divided between them. Sprinkle the sliced spring onions and the herbs into the soup and serve.

Marinated Thai chilli beef ☀

This delicious dish is great as a starter.

Serves 4

> 500g trimmed beef fillet
>
> 4 tablespoons sesame oil

for the dressing

> 1 clove of garlic, peeled
>
> 2 fresh red chillies
>
> a small bunch of fresh mint, leaves picked
>
> a small bunch of fresh coriander, leaves picked
>
> the juice of 1 lime
>
> 1 tablespoon Japanese rice vinegar
>
> 2 tablespoons Thai fish sauce
>
> a tablespoon sugar

To make the dressing, chop the garlic and chillies finely and mix them in a bowl with the mint, coriander, lime juice, vinegar, fish sauce and sugar.

Slice your beef fillet into as thin slices as you can and lay all the slices out on a serving dish, trying not to overlap them if possible. Spoon the dressing evenly over the beef and leave to marinate for a good hour. You'll see the lime and vinegar in the dressing start to slightly cook the beef.

Heat the sesame oil in a saucepan until hot, then pour it carefully over the marinated beef. Leave for 2 or 3 minutes for all the flavours to mix before serving.

4

world food

Pyrénées
3h/\\TS
39.95 €/kg

By late 2000 I had been working solidly for twelve years, playing Ricky Butcher in *EastEnders*. Even though I'd been having breaks, and the chance for holidays and weekends away, I was starting to feel like I'd been working hard on the one character for a long time. For many years Ricky had been one of the main characters in the show, so the workload was quite intensive at times. I spent most of the week on set and also had a lot of lines to learn. In many ways, I did enjoy playing Ricky and I realize it's unusual for a character to go on for such a long time on television. It meant I was financially secure and was starring in the biggest show in the UK. Yet I was also aware that the character couldn't go on for ever and I also felt that I needed a break. I worried that because I'd been so well known for one particular character it wouldn't necessarily be easy to know where to go next, acting-wise. I started a new relationship with a girl and we fell in love and decided to go travelling. We ended up travelling around the world for two years.

A Chinese friend of mine in London, called Geoff, knew I was going travelling and told me to hook up with a friend of his in Malaysia. So I met up with his friend, also called Geoff, in Kuala Lumpur. It's a great city. Geoff had grown up in England, but his family was Malaysian and so he decided to move back there. When I got to Malaysia, Geoff opened my eyes to loads of stuff. The best thing about the country is the good mixture of foods – they've got Indian, Chinese, Malay. He took us out every single night and as I was there for a couple of weeks, we tried loads of different restaurants. We had such a good time with him that we went back more than once to stay with him.

Throughout my travelling experiences I was trying traditional Chinese dishes, Malay dishes and Indian dishes and most of it was street cooking.

South-east Asian sea bass with chilli noodles and pak choi

Serves 4

For the fish

vegetable oil

4 x 200g fillets of sea bass

a small bunch of spring onions

1 fresh red chilli, finely sliced

2 cloves of garlic

a small bunch of fresh coriander, leaves picked

4 tablespoons Thai fish sauce

For the pak choi

sesame oil

1 clove of garlic, sliced

4 heads of pak choi

100ml chicken stock or water

oyster sauce

For the chilli noodles

sesame oil

2 cloves of garlic, peeled and chopped

a small piece of ginger, peeled and chopped

1 fresh red chilli, finely sliced

400g ready-cooked egg noodles

Scott showing me how it's done

Preheat your oven to 220°C/425°F/gas mark 7.

Tear four sheets of foil a little bit bigger than a double page of this book. Rub the middle of each sheet with a little vegetable oil and lay a piece of fish on top. Slice the spring onions thinly on the diagonal into long strips. Lay some of the spring onions on top of each piece of fish and sprinkle with the chilli and garlic. Spoon 1 tablespoon of soy sauce on top and wrap each piece of fish up in the foil, leaving a little space inside each parcel for the fish to steam.

Place the parcels on a baking tray and cook in the preheated oven for about 10 minutes.

Heat a saucepan and add a splash of sesame oil and the garlic. When the

163

garlic starts to sizzle, add the pak choi and fry for a minute on each side. Pour in the stock or water and simmer until the water has reduced almost to nothing and the pak choi is cooked through. Pour a little oyster sauce over the top and take off the heat.

To cook the chilli noodles, heat a non-stick frying pan and add a splash of sesame oil, the garlic, ginger and chilli. When they're sizzling, add the noodles and a little water. Stir and fry for a few minutes, until the noodles are warmed through and the water has all been absorbed.

Carefully remove the tray from the oven and unwrap the fish. Check that it's hot all the way through – if it is, it's cooked. Serve the fish with the coriander leaves, pak choi and the hot chilli noodles. Season if necessary.

Chicken and butternut squash curry ☼☼

This is my own version of Thai and Indian, though more on the Indian side. When you measure the rice and water, make sure you use the same size cup – it's a volume measurement.

Serves 2

    2 nice big chicken breasts, skin off

    2 teaspoons garam masala

    1 teaspoon ground ginger

    1 teaspoon ground coriander

    1 teaspoon curry powder

    1 teaspoon hot chilli powder (optional)

    1 clove of garlic, peeled and chopped

    1 small fresh red chilli, chopped

    olive oil

    ½ butternut squash

    1 onion, peeled and sliced

    1 x 400ml tin of coconut milk

    salt and freshly ground black pepper

    a sprig of fresh coriander

For the rice

    1 cup of rice

    2 cups of water

Cut the chicken into chunks and place it in a large mixing bowl. Add all the spices, the garlic, the chilli and a good glug of olive oil. Mix everything together, cover and allow to marinade for at least a good couple of hours, the longer the better.

Cut the butternut squash in half and scoop out the seeds. Chop into even chunks about the same size as the chunks of chicken. Heat a large saucepan and add a little oil. Fry the butternut squash with the onion for 5 minutes or so, until everything's softened and starting to brown. Transfer the contents of the pan to a bowl, put the pan back on the heat and add the chicken. Fry the chicken pieces, adding a little more oil if necessary, for a few minutes, then tip the squash and onion back into the pan and cook for a further 5 minutes.

Put the rice and the water into another saucepan and bring to the boil without stirring. Turn the heat right down, cover with a lid and leave to simmer for about 15 minutes.

Add the coconut milk to the squash and chicken, and cook gently for 15 to 20 minutes. Check that the chicken is cooked through and the squash is soft, then taste and add more seasoning if you need to.

By now the rice should have absorbed all the water and be nice and fluffy. Spoon it on to four plates with the curry alongside, and serve drizzled with some olive oil and sprinkled with a little chopped coriander.

Oriental duck crêpes

These crêpes make a delicious snack.

For 2 generous crêpes

      1 quantity basic crêpe mixture (see page 259)

      1 breast of duck

      1 tablespoon honey

      1 tablespoon soy sauce

      salt and freshly ground black pepper

      $1/2$ cucumber

      3 spring onions

      1 good tablespoon hoi sin sauce

      crushed chillies (optional)

Pre-heat your oven to 200°C/400°F/gas mark 6.

With a sharp knife score the duck lightly two or three times, then rub in the honey and soy sauce, and season well with salt and pepper.

Get a large heavy frying pan hot and place your duck breast in it, skin side down. There's no need for oil, as there is enough fat in the skin. Cook the duck for about 5 minutes until skin goes brown, then turn and cook for a further 3 minutes. With a spatula or a pair of kitchen tongs, lift the duck breast out of the frying pan and on to a baking tray skin side up. Pop it into the preheated oven for 10 minutes, or 15 minutes if you like your duck well done.

Take the duck out of the oven and let it sit for 5 minutes, then slice it fairly finely, across the breast, with a good sharp knife to avoid separating the skin from the meat. If you feel the duck isn't cooked through enough for your taste (I like mine kind of medium-rare, but everyone's different) just pop the slices back in a frying pan for a minute or so, until they've browned up a bit more.

Peel your cucumber, slice it in half lengthways and scoop out the seeds with a teaspoon. Cut the cucumber into batons as thinly as you can and finely chop your spring onions.

Make a crêpe according to the method on page 259. Spread the hoi sin sauce evenly over it while it's still in the pan, then add half of your sliced duck, cucumber and spring onions, leaving room on all sides for folding. If you're like me and like a bit of spice, shake over some chilli flakes. Fold the crêpe in half, and in half again and serve. Put the pan straight back on the stove to cook the second crêpe. You won't be disappointed.

People would go out and eat an evening meal and they would always stop after being on the booze and go to the proper traditional Chinese restaurants at three o'clock in the morning. They were packed! Singapore and Malaysian friends introduced me to Chinese food that you would never believe . . . Chinese people born in England have probably never even heard of most of it.

It was mainly very healthy food, a lot of steamed stuff. But then again, some of it was quite fatty, like the crispy pork. But I was open to trying anything. My approach to food would be that I would try anything once.

After Malaysia my girlfriend wanted to go and see her dad in Australia, on Magnetic Island, so we stayed there for a while. It was my first time in Australia and the seafood was great. They have these things called Moreton Bay bugs, which are a cross between a shrimp and a lobster tail, and they're quite a delicacy there, in Queensland especially. I enjoyed experimenting and tasting new seafoods that you won't find anywhere in the UK.

I've had three fairly lengthy trips to Australia in my life so far. I went to a place called Byron Bay for the first time about six years ago. It was there that I got into juicing fruits for breakfast. I used to have wheat grass shots, which

were quite nasty. Wheat grass is very strong, though apparently it's very good for you. You would have a little shot of wheat grass and then a juice, in the morning, and that would be your breakfast.

As I discovered more of Australia, I decided to try eating kangaroo, something I thought I'd never do. But meat is meat, and I was actually very surprised because it was nice and tender, like a fillet steak. The Aussies tend to cook kangaroo on the barbie. In fact, they sling anything on the barbie, like fish and prawns. Very similar to English food in a way, but obviously different meats and produce. I've tried ostrich, crocodile, kangaroo, possum. Crocodile's really nice actually – a cross between swordfish and chicken. It's lovely plainly grilled or fried, with a squeeze of lemon.

We didn't get into the barbie thing that much. We tried it once or twice, but I'm not a big barbie person. I prefer cooking in the kitchen. I find you don't have a lot of control over the food on a barbie. Everything tends to have the same sort of burnt taste.

Juices ☼

If you've got a juicing machine, it's really easy to make all kinds of juices that are delicious and really, really good for you. If vegetable juice doesn't sound too tasty to you, remember that by blending veg with fruit in the right way you can get pretty tasty results and have the best of both worlds.

Prepare fruit like apples and pears for juicing by coring them and cutting them into quarters. Carrots can be peeled (or not, if they're organic) and other root veg like beetroot peeled and cut into chunks. Ginger can be used as it is, just cut into chunks, and celery just broken into sticks. Citrus fruit has to be halved and squeezed first, before it's poured into the machine, and bananas have to be peeled.

If you like your juices with a thicker consistency, a ripe banana works wonders!

Serves 2

For apple and pear juice, use 4 apples and 2 pears.

For orange, apple, carrot and beetroot juice, use the juice of 2 oranges, with 2 apples, 3 carrots, and a beetroot.

For orange and grapefruit juice, use the juice of 4 oranges and 2 grapefruits.

For strawberry, raspberry, blackberry and banana juice, use a whole punnet of strawberries, green tops on, 2 punnets of raspberries and blackberries and 2 bananas.

For orange, apple and carrot juice, use 3 oranges, 1 apple and 4 carrots.

For Sid's special carrot juice, use 8 carrots and a small knob of root ginger.

For liver flush, (for the morning after) use the juice of 6 oranges, a small knob of ginger, a clove of garlic, a glug of olive oil and a pinch of cayenne pepper.

Place a jug under the spout of your juicing machine and start whizzing.

In 2001 I went to Greece for my brother Scott's wedding. I was only there for five days but in that time I experienced a lot of outdoor eating and a lot of mezze. We tended to eat at the hotel or at a little restaurant opposite, which did fresh fish, especially prawns. The Greeks like their prawns. And they have lovely produce – huge tomatoes, big cucumbers, even their breads taste amazing. You'd have a kebab there and instead of being greasy, it would be fresh grilled chicken and lots of vegetables diced up, cucumbers, tomatoes, aubergines and hot jalapeño peppers, all sorts of salads all mixed in. And you'd have a garlicky yoghurt dip called tsatziki. And that was just an ordinary bog-standard kebab! If you compare that to what we consider to be kebabs, it was actually quite a healthy meal. The lovely thing about the Greek restaurants was that the fish came straight from the sea and the menu was adapted to whatever fish had been caught.

When I was in New York, I enjoyed going to the delis; there's one on nearly every street corner. What I love about it is that if people are a bit indecisive about what they want to eat, they can just go in and buy something, and can even create their own dishes. For instance, in one deli there was a Chinese counter, a sushi counter, a pizza counter, a salad counter, a sandwich and wrap counter and a pasta counter. I'm surprised we don't have them like that in this country. They call the delis the melting point of all the different nationalities and backgrounds of New York. People are all merged together in the deli culture, the taste of so many different cuisines. I've also eaten in the New York Palace Hotel, which is Michelin-starred, very fancy and great to experience. Michelin star food is something I treat myself to once every couple of months. It's worth a little treat. I couldn't get used to the massive portions in New York, though. It's pretty scary, really. I think a lot of people over there are used to such portions, but each one would literally serve three people.

In Los Angeles I got into the whole clean eating thing – yeah, from one extreme to the other, but that's America for you! A lot of people talk about the huge contrast in America between the obsessively fit and the hugely overweight. I was struck by that as I walked around the streets. There's not a lot of middle ground. On the one hand, some people are eating huge portions and it's all buy-one-get-one-free and everything on discount, and on the other hand, you've got these restaurants in California that serve minuscule portions of ultra-clean food, like three baby carrots and a sliver of steamed fish and some zero-fat coriander foam and they charge the earth for it. I did find this little organic vegan restaurant and went there four times, for lunch. It was nice, healthy, different food too. Just vegetables, and you didn't feel hungry afterwards.

Greek salad ☀

Serves 4

> 200g mixed leaf salad
>
> 1 small red onion, finely sliced
>
> 1 red pepper, cored and sliced
>
> 1 green pepper, cored and sliced
>
> a handful of black olives, stoned
>
> 4 ripe vine tomatoes, roughly chopped
>
> balsamic and olive oil dressing (see page 129)
>
> 100g feta cheese
>
> salt and freshly ground black pepper
>
> a few sprigs of fresh flat-leaf parsley, leaves picked
>
> a few sprigs of fresh coriander, leaves picked

Put the salad leaves in a mixing bowl with the onion, peppers, olives and tomatoes and pour the balsamic dressing over the top. Crumble the feta cheese into the salad and season with a little salt and pepper, but be careful with the salt, as feta can be a bit salty.

Chop the parsley and coriander leaves and add to the salad. Toss everything together gently to stop the cheese breaking up too much, and serve in a big bowl.

Griddled halloumi with beetroot ☼

You can use precooked beetroot for this starter, the kind you get in a vacuum pack in the supermarket, but if you can get hold of some raw ones, scrub them and boil them yourself.

Serves 2

> olive oil
>
> 200g halloumi cheese, cut into good thick slices
>
> dried red chilli flakes
>
> 2 cooked beetroot
>
> 200g mixed salad leaves
>
> 1 lemon, cut in half
>
> salt and freshly ground black pepper

Preheat a griddle pan until hot, and add a little olive oil. Lay the slices of cheese in it, sprinkle with chilli flakes and cook for 2–3 minutes each side.

Slice the beetroot and toss with the salad leaves, the juice of 1/2 the lemon, a glug of olive oil and a pinch of salt and pepper. Squeeze the other lemon half over the hot grilled halloumi, and serve with the salad.

Sid's special tsatziki

½ a cucumber

450g Greek yoghurt

1 clove of garlic, peeled

salt and freshly ground black pepper

a small bunch of fresh mint

extra virgin olive oil

paprika (optional)

Peel the cucumber and slice it in half lengthways. With a teaspoon, scoop out the seeds from the inside and throw them away. Chop the cucumber finely and put into a bowl. Add the yoghurt and garlic and season well with salt and pepper. Chop the mint leaves and stir them in with a good glug of olive oil. Spoon into a serving bowl and serve sprinkled with a little paprika if you like.

We went to a famous Chinese restaurant, but to be honest, it wasn't fantastic. I had so many great experiences in Asia, it's difficult now for me to find a decent south-east Asian, Thai or Chinese restaurant in Europe or America. I reckon you shouldn't bother in Europe unless it's really highly recommended. Better making your own! Or eating local, traditional food.

I sometimes think that people from more ordinary, working backgrounds almost feel it's a bit poncey to cook differently from the normal British way of doing things. Even when travelling, people sometimes associate experimenting with food with being in some way pretentious. My interest has always been more about discovering the kind of 'normal' food people eat in different countries, made with basic ingredients, whether it's from Thailand, Malaysia, America, Australia, or France. Most of the food in this book is food that ordinary people eat in these countries, and there's nothing pretentious about that.

Most of us have been to Spain, it's part of our culture, it's the most common place to go on holiday. But a lot of people tend to go there and still stick to what they know. You can understand that – people work hard, they get their two weeks' holiday, and they just want to relax, get the sun, eat something tasty. They maybe don't want to experiment with local food in case they don't like it, and they might think: why try the local stuff when there's perfectly good British food, and the place is set up to feed us with what we know? People sometimes worry about getting a dicky tummy if they try something spicy or garlicky for the first time. But when you think about it, the takeaways you have at home from an Indian or Chinese restaurant are full of garlic and spices. All these restaurants have flourished, selling food that's more British than British. Bangers and mash and whatever. I'd like to encourage people to experiment, just take a little step beyond that and try some of proper Spanish food. What is there to be frightened of? The last thing I would do if I was in Spain would be to go and have steak and chips or pie and chips.

Proper Spanish restaurants are not that hard to find, and are often much cheaper than the stuff they set up for the British tourists. There are particular dishes that are a good first step for people who have never experienced Spanish food before. For example, if you like your fish and chips, there are Spanish recipes using just the same ingredients. Tastes great, makes a nice change, but nothing radical. I go to one restaurant out there where they bake fish and potatoes together. They slice the potatoes quite thinly, parboil them, add some onions, a bit of pepper, then lay them out on a baking tray and add a nice bit of fish with some garlic, olive oil and lemon and slow bake it – that's it, plain and simple - but absolutely delicious. The potatoes get really tasty from the olive oil and the fish juices. Understanding how to cook and how to get the best out of the ingredients is something we can all learn from southern Europe.

With wines I try to follow the same principle as food – when I'm travelling I drink whatever the local people drink. If you stick with the wine from the region, it tends to go well with the local food. Every time I'm in Spain, the only wine I drink is Rioja, it works really well with the tapas. And in Italy I drink Chianti if I'm eating something meaty, or maybe a Valpolicello with something lighter. Obviously, living in France, the best and biggest wine region in the world, I will only drink French wines, and it's reasonably priced as well. And staying local is better for the environment – it's important for people to try to source and eat locally.

Baked dorada Spanish style (posh fish and chips)

Serves 4

    2 whole dorada or bream, about 800g each

    1kg of potatoes, peeled and sliced thickly

    salt and freshly ground black pepper

    olive oil

    2 cloves of garlic, peeled and sliced

    2 Spanish onions, peeled and sliced

    juice of 1 lemon

    2 tablespoons white wine vinegar

    a few sprigs of fresh flat-leaf parsley, chopped

Preheat your oven to 200°C/400°F/gas mark 6.

When you buy your bream, make sure they're nice and fresh and get the fishmonger to scale them, gut them and cut the gills out.

Put the potatoes into a saucepan and cover with cold salted water. Bring to the boil and simmer gently until the potatoes are almost cooked, then drain well in a colander.

Place another saucepan on the heat and add a splash of oil. Add the garlic and onions and cook gently for about 10 minutes or so, until they're soft and sweet. Season with a few pinches of salt and twists of pepper.

Wash the bream inside and out and pat them dry with kitchen paper. Lay them on a chopping board. With a sharp knife, slash them three or four times on each side. Season them well with salt and pepper, and drizzle with olive oil and lemon juice.

Put half the cooked onions into an ovenproof baking dish and stir in the cooked drained potatoes. Season with salt and pepper. Spread the potatoes out so they're in an even layer, then lay the fish on top, side by side. Spoon the rest of the onions over the fish, cover with tinfoil and pop the dish into the preheated oven.

Bake for half an hour, then remove the foil and pour the vinegar around the fish, over the potatoes. Put the dish back into the oven, uncovered, for another 10 minutes. Check the fish is hot right the way through – if it is, it's cooked. Sprinkle with chopped parsley and serve the dish at the table for everyone to tuck in.

Boquerones

I love anchovies and I think this dish really helps to soften their saltiness. Great as a starter.

Serves 2

    12 nice fresh anchovies, filleted

    1 large clove of garlic, peeled

    a small bunch of fresh flat-leaf parsley

    salt and freshly ground black pepper

    1 tablespoon white wine vinegar

    3 tablespoons good olive oil

    dried chilli flakes (optional)

Arrange the anchovies side by side, silver side up, on a nice serving dish, trying not to overlap them too much. Chop the garlic and parsley finely and sprinkle them evenly over the fish. Season lightly with salt and pepper and drizzle with the vinegar and then the oil. Scatter some dried red chilli flakes over the top if you like a bit of a bite.

Leave to marinate for half an hour or so, then serve with nice crusty bread to soak up all the lovely oil and garlic.

After Australia, my girlfriend and I went to Bali. Bali was lovely, and introduced to me a whole different way of cooking. They'd cook fish on a barbecue with coconut shells, which was their so-called coal. They'd wrap the fish in a banana leaf and steam it on the barbecue, and serve it with plain rice and some morning glory – a vegetable similar to asparagus or broccoli. Green veg with a little marinade, soy sauce cum oyster sauce. There'd also be a side dish to mix with the fish, made up of spicy chillies and tamarind. Often British people travelling abroad are a bit nervous about trying anything other than meat and veg, or fish and chips. But for me, food was very much part of our travelling experience and learning about whichever country we were in. We were always trying to meet local people too. It's great to hook up and befriend people who have grown up in the area. Because I didn't know anyone in Bali, I paid a guy to drive us round for a couple of weeks, to take us to sightseeing places and good restaurants. This gave me a great start to finding out more about the country. You tend to find that there's a relationship between the climate and the food people eat. It can affect a lot of people's diet.

During our two years of travelling, we popped back to Europe periodically to see family and friends. By this point my girlfriend and I were getting quite serious, so we decided to spend a couple of months in France where she'd grown up. Her mum had a house down there in Aubeterre in the south-west, so we rented a place for ourselves nearby for a few months. I started to love the peace and tranquillity of the area and, of course, just being there with her.

At that point I agreed to do a one-off *EastEnders*

special. Although it was only a couple of weeks' filming, we both really missed France and realized we'd become quite attached to it. When we returned to the Aubeterre region after I'd finished filming in 2002, I decided to look into buying some property there. Initially I thought about buying a holiday home, but when I went to look at the properties in the area, I saw this restaurant for sale and ended up buying it! I didn't know a thing about restaurants, but I knew I loved food and this seemed like a way of pulling together everything I'd learned about cooking. So suddenly there I was, with a restaurant I'd bought on a whim. I thought, if it all fails, I could always lease it out. It was a nice opportunity anyway because it wasn't a huge investment, and I had a building at the end of it. It was something I really wanted to do.

The *EastEnders* special was a big success, and I'd agreed to go back to my role as Ricky Butcher full-time. But I wasn't sure how I felt about going back to the programme after so much time away, and especially having now bought the place in France. I had my brother Darren in France with me so he could

194

keep an eye on it while I was filming. We got the restaurant up and running and then I started working back in England, so all I was doing was flying back at the weekend and checking it out. Darren held the fort while I was away during the week, overseeing things. He's like me but a bit more erratic, but he got things up to a good standard there. Because I was so busy with work, I had to trust his judgement to know what a good bit of food was. He had already been learning about that, so I knew things were in safe hands.

The first summer we just opened, without renovating the building. The main aim was just to get the restaurant open and try to do the best we could. We gave it a lick of paint and I went out and bought more tables and chairs, just to make it look a bit nicer. But each year I took a slice of money from what we had earned and put it back into the restaurant to really get it up to scratch, which I eventually did before I sold it in 2006. It was small, but I had my own little touches in there to give it soul, like stuff I had from my own house that I thought would look good there. That, to me, was giving it the comfort zone, giving it the sort of atmosphere I liked myself, as if I was sitting at home, enjoying some food and wine.

I quickly found that there was a good sense of community in Aubeterre. Running a restaurant can be a surprisingly good way of getting to know the locals. People are really interested in what you're trying to do in any new venture. There is a frustrating

amount of bureaucracy in France, as anyone who has tried to start a business there will tell you, but people who'd been through it themselves were happy to give me tips on how to cut through the red tape. In fact, I soon found out that bureaucratic nightmares are a great topic of conversation in France, just like the weather is in Britain, and people love to compete with each other with endless horror stories.

I also started formulating ideas about the kind of food I wanted to serve, drawing on my travelling experiences. At that time, the menu pretty much covered everything I liked to eat. The restaurant was an investment, but I'd always enjoyed food and cooking it, so in a way it was a dream come true for me. I wrote the menu and chose everything down to the knives and forks and the whole ambience of the place. The menu

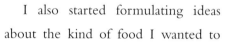

included dishes from Italy, Thailand, the Mediterranean, and even England. That was probably a bit of a risk – in a typical French village – but somehow it worked.

Spending time in France meant I got to learn a lot about French food. And the more I cooked, the more I enjoyed it, and I began to think that maybe I could really make something of the restaurant. It was exciting, but at the same time it was nerve-racking. I knew that a lot of people have exactly the same dream, but most of them fail, and I would have to be very lucky for it to have any success. I wanted to keep it all very quiet from the media back home, because if I were to fail I'd want to do it in private. I had to be confident enough to hope that all the experience I'd built up over the years would be enough to make a success out of it.

By this point, I was enjoying the restaurant more than I was enjoying

EastEnders, and I thought that I was missing out being away from France. The first summer I wasn't there, but the second summer I was, and I took full control. You can't understand about a restaurant unless you're there witnessing people's reactions, seeing what they like. Apart from knowing that the menu works, you also need to see the plates coming up from the kitchen, going on to the tables, getting feedback from customers and stuff like that. It was hard work and a huge learning curve. After the first year, my brother Darren took control during the week, and I would come over at weekends and step in. I picked the chefs from a college and sort of trained them. Trained them in the way I wanted. If I wouldn't eat it, my customers wouldn't eat it.

The second year, when I finished work on *EastEnders*, I came back and devoted all my time to the restaurant for the next three years. I spent more time in the kitchen and was actually very hands-on. I loved the restaurant – it wasn't a huge project in the sense of the financial side of it, but it was a huge thing for me to do something by myself. It was something totally different from acting. I enjoy acting, but with the restaurant I was my own boss, I got everyone else to do *their* jobs. As opposed to being directed and learning your lines, I was doing the directing, and that was the challenge, to suddenly be in charge of everything, where the buck stops here. But it was good and most of the time things went pretty smoothly.

Asparagus and egg salad ☀☀

White asparagus in a jar is really quite nice if you can't find the real thing, and it makes knocking this salad together quick and easy. I like to use good eggs, free range and organic, for this dish – it makes a big difference to the flavour.

Serves 4

> 4 large eggs
>
> 200g mixed salad leaves
>
> a few cherry tomatoes, sliced in half
>
> 1 large carrot, peeled and grated
>
> a handful of olives, stoned
>
> a red onion, thinly sliced
>
> French dressing (see page 129)
>
> salt and freshly ground black pepper
>
> a jar of white asparagus, drained

My neighbour David with his hens

Bring a saucepan of water to the boil and carefully lower in the eggs. Bring back to the boil and cook for exactly 5 minutes. Lift out with a slotted spoon and place on a plate to cool. When they are cool enough to handle, carefully peel the shell off and put the eggs to one side.

Put the salad leaves into a bowl with the tomatoes, carrot, olives and onion. Add the French dressing and toss everything together. Season with salt and pepper, divide between four plates and lay the asparagus spears over the top. Carefully slice the eggs in half and place 2 halves on each plate of salad, with the yolk side facing upwards. They should be almost hardboiled, with the yolk just a little bit soft. Drizzle with a little olive oil and serve.

Tomato and onion salad

This is a good little salad to serve at a barbecue, or with some warm baked mackerel for lunch.

Serves 2

6 ripe vine tomatoes

1 red onion, peeled

balsamic and olive oil dressing (see page 129)

With a sharp knife, slice the tomatoes thinly and lay them out on a serving plate. Slice the onion as thinly as you can and scatter it over the tomatoes. Whiz up the dressing, spoon it over the tomatoes and onions and serve.

Roasted tomato and basil soup

Serves 4

> 6 nice big juicy tomatoes
>
> 1 clove of garlic, peeled
>
> a few fresh basil leaves
>
> olive oil
>
> balsamic vinegar
>
> salt and freshly ground black pepper
>
> 565ml chicken or vegetable stock
>
> 2–3 tablespoons double cream

Preheat your oven to 220°C/425°F/gas mark 7.

With a small sharp knife, cut the green stalks out of the tops of the tomatoes, leaving a small hole. Slice the garlic into 6 pieces and place a piece in each of the holes with a basil leaf. Push them down inside the tomato a bit so they don't fall out.

Place the tomatoes on a small baking tray, drizzle them with olive oil and balsamic vinegar and sprinkle them with salt and pepper. Place the tray in the preheated oven for about 20–30 minutes, checking now and then to make sure they don't burn.

Tip the tomatoes and all the sticky juices from the roasting tray into a food processor and blitz until smooth. Pour through a sieve into a clean saucepan, pressing with the back of a wooden spoon or spatula to make sure you get all the juice. Add the stock, then place the pan on the heat and bring to the boil. Add a bit more salt and pepper and simmer on a low heat for 7–10 minutes. Stir in the cream 2 minutes before the end of cooking and serve.

204

Rustic Camembert dip with honey, thyme and garlic

This can be a nice starter, or part of a mezze platter, or even the cheese course at a dinner party.

Serves 2 to 4

 1 x 250g whole Camembert cheese, the kind you buy in a little
  wooden box

 1 clove of garlic, finely sliced

 a few small sprigs of fresh thyme

 1 tablespoon runny honey

Preheat your oven to 150°C/300°F/gas mark 2.

Remove the Camembert from its box, take it out of its wrapping, and place it back in the box. Pierce the skin of the cheese with the tip of a knife, and push slivers of garlic and sprigs of thyme into the holes. Drizzle some honey over the top, put the lid of the box back on, and cook in the oven for 15–18 minutes.

Serve warm, with some crusty French bread to dip through the skin of the camembert into the soft warm cheese underneath.

Sid's special chopped tomato relish

This is easier to make if you have a nice big board and a good chopping knife. It's great spooned on to steaks or grilled fish.

Makes a nice bowlful

1 red onion

4 ripe vine tomatoes

½ a cucumber, peeled, halved and seeds scraped out

a few sprigs of fresh coriander

extra virgin olive oil

lemon juice

salt and freshly ground black pepper

white wine vinegar

Chop the onion on a large clean chopping board, then add the tomatoes, cucumber and coriander and chop everything together. Scrape the chopped vegetables into a bowl and add a glug of olive oil, a squeeze of lemon juice and a good few pinches of salt and pepper. Before serving it, I like to add a few drops of white wine vinegar just to give it a bit of a kick.

Danielle Petet the butterfly man

206

Chargrilled aubergines and courgettes

Serves 6

> 1 aubergine
>
> 3 courgettes
>
> olive oil
>
> salt and freshly ground black pepper
>
> wine vinegar
>
> a few sprigs of fresh flat-leaf parsley, chopped

With a sharp knife, slice your aubergine into rounds 1cm thick and your courgette into lengthways slices about as thick as a pound coin. Lay them out on a clean work surface, brush them on both sides with a little olive oil and season with salt and pepper.

Heat a griddle pan until it's nice and hot and cook your vegetables for about 2–3 minutes on each side. You will probably have to do this in batches.

Lay your cooked aubergine and courgette out on a serving plate, drizzle with a little vinegar and olive oil and scatter with the chopped parsley before serving.

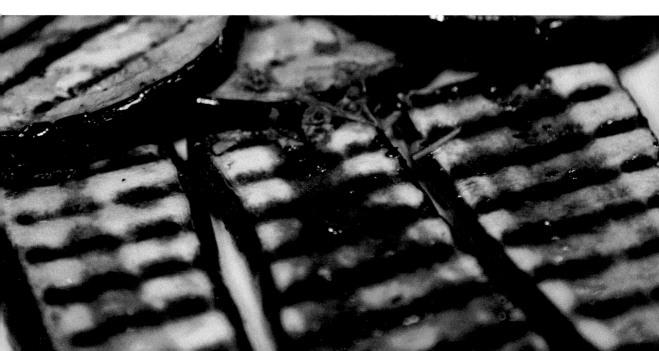

All my time was given over to the restaurant. I enjoyed the social life that went with it, but more than anything I loved being in the kitchen and learning about the food and how to cook everything, so I could step in at any point and help out. The staff knew that I understood about food so they knew what sort of standard I expected from the kitchen. I did all the buying in the first couple of years. I would buy the best meat and veg I could find in the area. It was exciting, learning and perfecting more dishes. You can spend a lot of time in the kitchen and cook the same stuff over and over again, but once you have got a lot more ingredients in front of you, you can play about with them and make it better. So that was my big learning curve, having all this produce to play with and trying to motivate the chefs as well.

I sourced produce from different people in the local area, because although

out there a lot of people grew their own stuff, nine times out of ten they grew too much for their own use, so they sold it on. I got friendly with a couple called David and Gina, who were regulars in the restaurant. They are a lovely couple, a retired builder and his wife; they'd moved to the countryside to take things easier, but David is a bit of a workaholic and soon started doing building for half the village. They used to bring me a lot of tomatoes and herbs from their garden. I also got to know this guy, Danielle Petet, who I called the Butterfly Man as he owned the butterfly museum opposite my restaurant. He basically came to me and said he had loads of produce to sell. I think he might have supplied the previous owners. Apart from being good local organic produce, it was also cheap. I'd rather barter with someone who has taken the time to care and look after their goods, so to speak.

Summer fruit salad

When you're making a simple fruit salad, it's important that you use really good ripe fruit. Have a look around for the best stuff, taste before you buy, and try to find fruit that has been grown locally. Fruit loses its sweetness if it's been off the bush in a punnet for a while.

In summer try to use things like strawberries and other red fruit, melons, and plums, and at other times of the year use things like kiwi and banana.

Chop the fruit up into nice small chunks, arrange it on plates, and dress it with live natural yoghurt, a squirt of fresh runny honey and a little bit of mint.

If your fruit isn't as ripe and sweet as it could be, sometimes it's nice to soak it in a glass of freshly squeezed orange juice for half an hour before serving it.

Melon with pinot rouge

Serves 4

    2 small ripe melons

    1 bottle of Pinot Rouge

Slice the melons in half crossways, then scoop out the seeds and throw them away. Trim the ends of the melons flat so they sit nicely on a plate. Place them on a tray and fill half full of Pinot Rouge. Carefully place the tray in the fridge and chill for about an hour. Serve cold.

Chocolate and banana crêpes

For 2 generous crêpes

     1 quantity basic crêpe mixture (see page 259)

     2 tablespoons chocolate spread

     2 bananas, thinly sliced

Peel the banana and slice into thin pieces. Make a crêpe according to the method on page 259. Once it's almost cooked on both sides, spread a good dollop of chocolate spread evenly over the side facing you, while it's still in the pan, and add your sliced banana, leaving room on all sides for folding. Fold the crêpe in half and serve. Put the pan straight back on the stove to cook the next crêpe.

Poached pears with chocolate sauce

Serves 4

> 4 pears
>
> 500g caster sugar
>
> 1 vanilla pod
>
> 150g dark chocolate
>
> 1 tablespoon butter
>
> 200ml double cream

Trim the bottoms of your pears flat with a sharp knife so they stand up straight without wobbling. Peel them with a vegetable peeler and sit them in a small saucepan. Try to find one that fits them as snug as possible. Scatter the sugar over the top and add just enough cold water to cover them. Slit the vanilla pod down the middle and with a teaspoon, scoop out the little black seeds from inside. Put the seeds and the empty pod into the water with the pears and place the pan on the heat.

Bring to the boil and simmer gently for 5 to 10 minutes, until you can push a knife into a pear easily. Turn the heat off and leave the pears to cool down slightly in the syrup.

Break the chocolate into little chunks and place in a heatproof bowl with the butter and cream. Fill

a saucepan half full of hot water and place on the heat. Sit the bowl over the saucepan and make sure the bottom of it isn't touching the surface of the water – if it is, pour a little water out of the pan. Melt the chocolate and butter into the cream, stirring all the time. As soon as the sauce is smooth, use a pair of oven gloves to lift the bowl off the saucepan – watch out for steam coming out from underneath!

Lift the pears out with a slotted spoon and place them in four separate bowls. Pour the hot chocolate sauce over the top and serve.

The Butterfly Man was passionate about his growing. He has a big set-up there and grows quite a lot of different stuff. From Easter, certain things would be in season early on. Beautiful salad stuff, lettuces, herbs, a good crop of berries later on in the summer. (I get a massive crop of cherries in my own garden in June. I don't have much of a sweet tooth myself, but I like to put them on as a garnish. It livens things up.) From July, the Butterfly Man has the most incredible crop of all kinds of different tomatoes. He's extremely proud of them, and develops varieties from seeds sourced from various corners of the globe. He's obsessed with his growing and very proud of his seeds. In fact, if you get him started on his seeds, you'll be there all day.

His other big passion was butterflies. He used to go off travelling in the winter and he would do three or four months in Africa, South America, all over the world, catching butterflies to put in his museum. He used to get bugs and snakes and reptiles as well. He is just an all-round passionate and eccentric

guy. My French wasn't great to start with, and his English wasn't much better, but we managed to muddle along pretty well. He regularly gave me salads: lettuces, tomatoes and a lot of fresh herbs, hard to get in the local shops, which were all quite small. I tried to go cash and carry for the bulk, like the drinks, but I'd try and source everything else from local farmers. The meat came from the abattoir and the ducks came from the duck farm.

David also used to give us a load of eggs. Great eggs, David and Gina's. He really loves his hens. You can tell by the way he looks at them! But sourcing good products was all a case of trial and error. I was always looking for the best I could buy. I found a little fruit and veg market. It was a good set-up, but some things were just not as nice as the local ones. There's nothing like having someone local, someone there hand-picking the fruit and veg personally and bringing you the best.

Cherry clafoutis

This is a classic French dessert and I love to cook it with the cherries from my garden in France.

Serves 6 to 8

> 450g fresh stoned cherries
>
> 285ml milk
>
> 3 eggs
>
> 150g granulated sugar
>
> 1 teaspoon vanilla extract
>
> 200g plain flour
>
> 2 teaspoons baking powder
>
> icing sugar for dusting
>
> double cream or crème fraiche to serve

Heat the oven to 180°C/350°F/gas mark 4.

Butter a shallow baking pan and put in the cherries. Bake in the oven for 15 minutes and remove once done.

Meanwhile, combine the milk, eggs, sugar, vanilla, flour and baking powder in a mixing bowl and whisk the mixture by hand until all the ingredients are well combined and the batter is smooth.

Butter a separate shallow baking dish (a 25cm quiche dish would be ideal) and pile in half the cherries. Pour the batter mixture over, then drop in the remaining cherries and bake in the oven for 40 minutes.

Once cooked, sprinkle with icing sugar and serve hot or cold with fresh double cream or crème fraiche.

a french
adventure

I had a great team of chefs at the restaurant, but one weekend there were staffing problems and I had to do all the cooking myself. Luckily, it wasn't too busy. So I thought, 'What'll I do? I might as well give it a try myself. It can't be that bad, I can cook.' I kept the menu to four starters and four mains and a few desserts and ended up cooking on my own all weekend for about forty covers a night. Just me and a waitress, and it went well. There were a few teething problems, a few panic moments. I remember on the first day I was trying to do a starter and a couple of mains and working on a dessert at the same time, and I forgot about a piece of fish that I'd put in the oven. I pulled it out without a glove. I burnt my hand and screamed the house down, flung the fish in the air and it all went on the floor. That was pure pressure! But as the second day went on, I got used to it.

The back of the restaurant and the flats above

At first the restaurant was almost a novelty thing, but when I got into it, I realized what a big part of my life it had become. We went through teething problems, of course, nothing major, but things that were outside my normal experience. Sometimes I'd think, do I really need this hassle? But then I'd remember the good times, whether I was working or sitting there myself watching people enjoying their meals. Putting smiles on their faces. I've always looked on food as a great thing to share with other people.

Regular customers are important, because it's good to get feedback from them about the various dishes on the menu. And, thankfully, we had quite a few regulars who would come once or twice a week. They became good friends – and good critics too, sometimes. And as well as the regulars we got customers from all walks of life – English Dutch, Germans, Americans and quite a few French people too, because it was different from what they were used to. A lot of the restaurants in France tend to do the same food. We did the classic dishes, but we also did something a little bit different. We stuck to a good-quality rustic menu, dishes from around the world, with good produce being the main theme. The local restaurants, I remember, were either quite prissy Michelin-starred and very expensive, or Harvester-type places. We were somewhere in between, like a gastro bar. Sometimes I'd arrange a Mexican night, or sometimes Thai. I also had a friend who would come in and make really good Indian curry, which was a whole new experience for the French community. It was quite unique for the area, for anywhere in rural France at all really. Where else could you find pâté alongside Thai fish cakes, or Parma ham with melon, or something quite English?

Thai prawn curry with turmeric rice ⚜

Serves 4

    1 red pepper, halved, seeds removed

    1 yellow pepper, halved, seeds removed

    3 cloves of garlic, peeled

    2.5cm of fresh ginger, peeled

    a stick of lemon grass, cut into pieces

    1 fresh red chilli

    a small bunch of fresh basil

    a small bunch of fresh coriander

    1 x 400ml tin of coconut milk

    a pinch of sugar

    1kg peeled fresh raw prawns

    Thai fish sauce

    a handful of raisins (optional)

For the rice

    1 cup of rice

    2 cups of water

    1 teaspoon of powdered turmeric

    1/2 a chicken stock cube

Put the rice, the 2 cups of water and the turmeric into a saucepan with the crumbled stock cube and bring to the boil without stirring. Turn the heat down, cover with a lid and leave to simmer for about 15 minutes.

Put the peppers, garlic, ginger, lemon grass, chilli, basil and coriander into the blender, keeping back a few herb leaves for garnishing later. Blitz everything together until smooth, and pour into a large saucepan. Place on the heat, bring to the boil and simmer gently for about 5 minutes. Add the coconut milk and the sugar and bring back to the boil.

By now the rice should have absorbed all the water and be nice and fluffy, so turn the heat off and put the lid on to keep it warm.

Drop the prawns into the sauce and season with a splash of fish sauce. Simmer for 5 minutes or so, until the prawns cook through, then add the raisins if you're using them and take the pan off the heat. Taste the sauce, and if it needs salt, add a few drops more of fish sauce. Scatter with your reserved leaves of coriander and basil, and serve with the turmeric rice.

Sid's fantastic Thai fishcakes ✳ ✳

I love to serve these fishcakes as a starter. Delicious!

Serves 2

 a small bunch of fresh coriander

 a small piece of fresh ginger, peeled

 1 stick of lemon grass, finely chopped

 1 clove of garlic, peeled

 2 fresh red chillies

 300g white fish, such as cod or monkfish

 6 uncooked tiger prawns, peeled

 1/2 teaspoon turmeric

 1 teaspoon ground cumin

 Thai fish sauce

 1 lime

 olive oil

Preheat your oven to 180°C/350°F/gas mark 4.

In a food processor, blitz the coriander, ginger, lemon grass, garlic and chillies. Add the fish and the prawns with the turmeric, cumin and a splash of fish sauce. Pulse the fish into the other ingredients until everything looks mixed but you can still see chunks of fish. It makes for a much more interesting texture, rather than the over-processed sponginess you sometimes get in fishcakes. Divide the mix into four and shape into fishcakes with your hands. If you wet your hands when you do this, they won't stick to the mixture too much. Place in the fridge for 30 minutes to bind the ingredients together.

Heat a 1cm covering of oil in a shallow non-stick ovenproof frying pan and have a plate lined with a few sheets of kitchen paper standing by. Carefully place the fishcakes into the oil, taking care that the oil doesn't splash your fingers, and fry them for a minute without turning them. Turn them carefully with a spoon or a pair of metal tongs and place the pan in the preheated oven for 7–10 minutes, until the fishcakes are hot and cooked through.

Lift the fishcakes out with a slotted spoon and drain on the kitchen paper. Serve hot, with chunks of lime to squeeze over the top, some chilli dressing (see page 129) and plenty of cold beer.

231

Breast of duck

Serves 4

> 4 breasts of duck
>
> 4 tablespoons runny honey
>
> salt and freshly ground black pepper
>
> 1 fresh red chilli, finely chopped (optional)

Preheat your oven to 200°C/400°F/gas mark 6.

With a sharp knife score the fatty skin of the duck breasts lightly in a criss-cross pattern. Try not to cut into the meat! Spread the honey over the duck, sprinkle with salt, pepper and chopped chilli if you like it hot, and rub the flavourings well into the scored skin and the meat.

Get a large heavy frying pan hot and place your duck breasts in it, skin side down. Cook for 3 or 4 minutes, then turn them over and cook for the same amount of time on the other side. With a spatula or a pair of kitchen tongs, lift the duck breasts out of the frying pan and on to a baking tray.

Bake them skin side up in the preheated oven for 10 minutes if you like your duck medium, then slice into pieces and serve. I love this dish with my potato gratin (page 236) and mixed veg side (page 29).

Potato gratin

Serves 4 to 6

> a knob of butter
>
> 2 cloves of garlic, peeled and finely crushed
>
> 1kg potatoes, peeled
>
> 400ml single cream
>
> 150g grated Parmesan cheese
>
> salt and freshly ground black pepper
>
> grated nutmeg

Preheat your oven to 180°C/350°F/gas mark 4.

Take a baking dish big enough to hold all your ingredients, rub the inside with the butter, and scatter the garlic evenly into it.

With a sharp knife, slice your potatoes as thinly as possible. Lay an even layer of the potato slices over the bottom of the dish and season them with salt and pepper. Pour some of the cream on top and sprinkle with Parmesan. Repeat this process until you've used up all your potatoes, cream and Parmesan. Sprinkle some grated nutmeg over the top and place in the preheated oven for 35–40 minutes, or until cooked through and golden brown on top.

Fillet of beef with Roquefort, chunky chips and pea purée

The key to a good steak is, of course, good-quality meat. I recommend finding a good butcher's shop where they hang their meat properly. The steaks might look a bit darker in colour, but they will be full of flavour and really tender and juicy. You can normally tell how done your steak is by prodding it with your finger. A raw steak is very soft and the more cooked a steak gets the firmer it becomes.

Serves 2

1 clove of garlic, peeled

salt and freshly ground black pepper

200g frozen peas

2 tablespoons crème fraiche

2 x 200g fillet steaks

olive oil

140ml single cream

100g Roquefort cheese, broken into pieces

Bring a saucepan of water to the boil with the garlic clove and a pinch of salt. Add the frozen peas and cook for 2–3 minutes. Drain them, then place them back in the empty saucepan. Add 1–2 spoonfuls of crème fraiche, then mash the peas with a masher and season with salt and pepper.

Before you cook your steaks, rub them with a little olive oil and sprinkle with salt and pepper. I sometimes like to massage a little balsamic vinegar into steak before I cook it, especially if I'm eating it plain, without a sauce. I think

this really helps to flavour and tenderize it even more.

Get a griddle pan nice and hot and put your steaks in. The cooking time for a steak depends on how thick it is, and how you like it cooked. With a good-sized fillet steak, I normally cook it for about 3–4 minutes on each side, then take it out of the pan and let it sit on a chopping board for about 5 minutes to let it rest. This helps the meat fibres relax a bit after cooking so it cuts easily. If you want it nice and hot on the plate, you can flash it for a few seconds in the hot griddle pan before you serve it.

To make the sauce, just warm the cream in a small saucepan and add the cheese. Once everything's bubbling, season with a little pepper – the Roquefort should be salty enough – and take off the heat.

Serve the steaks with the pea purée and a few chunky chips (see page 85), with the Roquefort sauce poured over the top.

Gina's brioche bread and butter pudding ☀☀

Serves 4

> 6 slices of brioche
>
> 50g unsalted butter
>
> 50g mixed sultanas and currants
>
> 40g caster sugar
>
> 3 egg yolks and 1 whole egg
>
> 300ml milk
>
> 300ml double cream

Spread the slices of brioche with the butter and cut into fingers or squares. Rub an ovenproof baking dish with a little butter and lay half the brioche slices in it. Sprinkle evenly with the dried fruit and half the sugar. Top with the remaining brioche slices, buttered side up, and sprinkle with the rest of the sugar.

Beat the egg yolks and whole egg together with the milk and cream, and pour through a sieve on to the pudding.

Set your oven to 160°C/325°F/gas mark 3, and leave the pudding to stand for 30 minutes while it heats up. Bake the pudding in the preheated oven for 45 to 50 minutes, until puffed and golden brown on top.

Parma ham and melon salad

Serves 4

> ½ a ripe melon, seeds scooped out
>
> 1 x 200g bag of mixed salad
>
> a handful of cherry tomatoes, sliced in half
>
> balsamic and olive oil dressing (see page 129)
>
> 12 slices of Parma ham

With a sharp knife, slice the melon into as many thin wedges as you can. Trim the skin off the slices if you like. Toss the mixed salad and the tomatoes with the balsamic dressing and divide between four plates. Lay the melon slices on the plates of salad, drape the Parma ham over the top and serve.

Mussels provençales ☀

These mussels are a real classic and great as a starter.

Serves 2

> 1kg mussels
>
> olive oil
>
> 1 small onion, peeled and chopped
>
> 2 cloves of garlic, peeled and chopped
>
> 1/2 a courgette, chopped
>
> 1 tablespoon dried Provençal herbs
>
> 1 x 400g tin of tomatoes
>
> salt and freshly ground black pepper
>
> 1 glass of dry white wine
>
> a small bunch of fresh flat-leaf parsley, chopped

Wash your mussels first in plenty of cold water, pulling off any beardy bits you find on them, and throw away any that aren't tightly closed.

Heat a large saucepan or wok and add a glug of olive oil. Add the chopped onion, garlic, courgette and herbs, and when they've fried for a couple of minutes, add the tomatoes and season well with salt and pepper. Simmer gently for 10 minutes, then add a good glass of dry white wine and the mussels.

Cover with a lid and cook for 5 minutes or so until most of the mussels have opened. Pick out any that haven't opened and throw them away. Sprinkle with the chopped parsley, and serve with another glug of olive oil and some crusty bread.

CHATEAU
2003
BERGERAC SEC
APPELLATION BERGERAC SEC
ALAIN MERILLIER
PROPRIÉTAIRE À GAGEAC ROUILLAC
DORDOGNE - FRANCE
MIS EN BOUTEILLE AU
13,5% vol.

Salade Niçoise ☼

Serves 2

2 good handfuls of mixed salad leaves

12 cherry tomatoes, cut in half

1/2 a red onion, peeled and thinly sliced

1 green or red pepper, cored and sliced

1 x 200g tin of tuna, drained

balsamic and olive oil dressing (see page 129)

a handful of black olives, stoned

2 eggs, hardboiled

Put your salad leaves into a bowl and add the tomatoes, onion and pepper. Flake the tuna into the bowl in even chunks, and toss the salad gently with the balsamic dressing and the olives.

Shell the eggs and cut each one into 4 pieces. Divide the salad between two shallow bowls, arrange the egg quarters evenly around the edge, drizzle with a little more oil and serve.

Sid's melanzane

Serves 4 to 6

> olive oil
>
> 2 cloves of garlic, peeled and chopped
>
> 1 tablespoon mixed Italian seasoning
>
> 1 x 700g jar of passata
>
> salt and freshly ground black pepper
>
> 2 aubergines
>
> a small bunch of fresh basil, leaves picked
>
> 4 balls of buffalo mozzarella, sliced
>
> grated Parmesan cheese

Preheat your oven to 180°C/350°F/gas mark 4.

Heat a saucepan and add a splash of olive oil and the garlic. Fry gently until light brown, then add the herbs and the tomato passata. Simmer for about 10 minutes and season with a little salt and pepper. Slice the aubergines lengthways into slices about 1cm thick, sprinkle them all over with salt and leave them for about an hour.

Wipe off the juices the salt has drawn out of the aubergines and pat them dry with kitchen paper. Heat a griddle pan over a medium heat and griddle the slices of aubergine a few at a time until nice and soft. Lay them on a tray to cool. Set aside a few leaves of basil for serving. Cover the bottom of an ovenproof baking dish with a layer of aubergine and put a layer of tomato sauce on top. Cover with a layer of basil, then a layer of mozzarella, and repeat until you've got about three layers of each. Sprinkle with some of the Parmesan and place the dish in the preheated oven for 20–25 minutes.

Sprinkle with fresh basil and more Parmesan before serving.

Darren's special poule au pot ❋ ❋ ❋

Serves 6

    1 onion

    3 carrots

    3 sticks of celery

    3 cloves of garlic

    2 whole leeks, trimmed and washed

    olive oil

    salt and freshly ground black pepper

    1 ½ glasses of white wine

    1 x 2.5kg cornfed chicken

    2 litres chicken stock

    1kg potatoes, peeled

    2 bay leaves

    1 bouquet garni (thyme, bay and a stick of celery)

Cut your onion, carrots, celery and leeks into big chunks roughly the same size and roughly chop the garlic. Heat a large deep saucepan, big enough to fit your chicken in, and add a splash of oil and all the chopped vegetables. Fry gently for a few minutes, adding a little salt and pepper, then add the wine. Cook for about 5 minutes, then put the chicken into the pan on top of the veg, cover with the stock and add the bay leaves.

Bring the stock to the boil and simmer over a low heat with a lid half on for about 2–2½ hours, depending on the size of your chicken.

Add the potatoes to the dish 40 minutes before serving. Cover with more stock if they are not fully submerged.

Once the chicken is well cooked through and the legs pull away from the body easily, turn the heat off and carefully lift the chicken out of the pan with tongs or a slotted spoon and on to a clean tray. It may break up as you try to pull it out of the pan, but don't worry too much about this, as you're going to strip the meat off the bones anyway.

Skim the fat off the top of the stock while the chicken cools a little, then pull the chicken off the bones. Get rid of the bones and the skin and the bits you're not going to eat, then place the chicken back in the stock, put the pan back on the heat and simmer for another 15 minutes or so to warm everything up before serving.

Scallops St Jacques

These scallops with leeks are great during the winter months.

Serves 2

2 leeks, trimmed and washed

500ml vegetable oil

salt and freshly ground black pepper

a good knob of butter

10 fresh scallops out of the shell

Cut off the green tops of the leeks and shred them with a sharp knife into long fine strips. Heat most of the vegetable oil in a saucepan and deep-fry a few spoonfuls of leek strips at a time, until they're golden brown and crispy. Lift out with a metal slotted spoon and drain on kitchen paper. Keep going until they're all done, then sprinkle with salt and put to one side.

Heat a saucepan and add the butter. Cut the whites of the leeks into chunks and toss them in the sizzling butter. Turn the heat down and cook them very gently so that they soften without going brown. Season with salt and pepper and keep warm.

Heat a large, heavy saucepan and add a splash of oil. Season the scallops well with salt and pepper and fry them for about a minute on each side in the hot pan. If the scallops are bigger than golfball size, they might need a minute or two longer to cook.

Spoon the soft leek whites on to two plates and arrange the scallops on top. Drop a pile of the fried crispy leeks on top of the scallops and serve.

Seared salmon with creamy dill sauce

Serves 4

For the creamy dill sauce

> olive oil
>
> 2 tablespoons white wine
>
> juice of 1/2 lemon
>
> 568ml single cream
>
> 2 tablespoons chopped fresh dill
>
> 1 tablespoon chopped fresh parsley
>
> salt and freshly ground black pepper

For the seared salmon

> olive oil
>
> 4 salmon fillets
>
> salt and freshly ground black pepper

Season the salmon fillets with salt and pepper. Heat a splash of oil in a large saucepan over a medium high heat. Add the wine and lemon juice and bring to the boil. Once boiled, add the cream and bring back to a simmer, then continue to cook until all the ingredients are well combined and the cream has reduced slightly. Stir in the dill and parsley and check the seasoning.

Heat a splash of oil in a large frying pan over a high heat and then add the salmon fillets. Sear them for 4–5 minutes, then turn over and cook for a further 3–4 minutes.

Serve the salmon fillets with the dill sauce, boiled new potatoes and some freshly boiled garden peas.

Creamy mushroom and parmesan side

Serves 4

a knob of butter

2 cloves of garlic, peeled and sliced

1 shallot, peeled and chopped

a few fresh chives, chopped

500g mushrooms, wiped and halved

180ml single cream

2 handfuls of grated Parmesan cheese

salt and freshly ground black pepper

a few sprigs of fresh flat-leaf parsley, chopped

Heat a saucepan big enough to hold all the ingredients and melt the butter in it. Add the garlic, shallot and chives and cook gently until softened. Throw in the mushrooms, turn the heat up and fry until they start to colour. Turn the heat down again and add the cream and the Parmesan. Season with salt and pepper and cook gently for about 5–7 minutes, until the sauce looks thick and creamy. Serve sprinkled with the parsley.

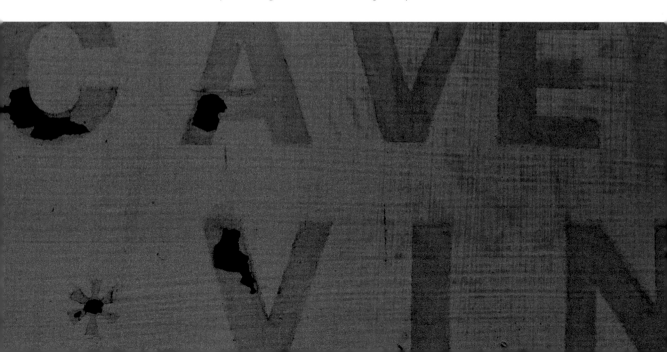

Mushroom and spinach crêpes

Since I've had my house in France I've got into crêpes in a big way. My mushroom and spinach version are a great snack, any time of day.

For 2 generous crêpes

For the crêpes

120g flour (buckwheat if available, plain if not)

a pinch of salt

1 egg

150ml milk

150ml water

1 tablespoon butter, plus extra for cooking the crêpes

For the filling

olive oil

a small knob of butter

1 small onion, peeled and chopped

a handful of mushrooms

salt and freshly ground black pepper

100g baby spinach

a few sprigs of fresh parsley, chopped

a few fresh chives, chopped

1 tablespoon crème fraiche

Sieve the flour and salt into a mixing bowl, then crack the egg in and give it a stir. Add the milk and water, stirring as you go. Melt the butter and add to

the bowl, then whisk it all up until smooth and creamy. Put to one side for half an hour or so while you make the filling.

Heat the oil and a knob of butter in a medium pan and fry off your onions and mushrooms for a few minutes, until softened. Season well with salt and pepper, then add a handful of baby spinach and cook for a further 3 – 4 minutes, stirring frequently.

Heat a small dash of olive oil in a frying pan. Ladle in some of your batter and swirl round until it thinly covers the pan. (You can make two generous-sized crêpes with this amount of batter.) Cook for 30–45 seconds, flipping the crêpe over so both sides are done.

While the crêpe is still in the pan, spread half of your crème fraiche over it, then add half the mushroom and spinach and a good sprinkle of parsley and chives, leaving room on all sides for folding. Fold the sides of the crêpe over the filling and serve. Do the same with a second crêpe. Pop a bit salad of your choice on the plate beside the finished crêpe if you fancy a nice added touch.

Minestrone soup ☀ ☀

This soup is delicious and seriously filling.

Serves 4 to 6

    olive oil

    a small red onion, finely chopped

    3 cloves of garlic, peeled and chopped

    a generous sprig of fresh thyme, leaves picked

    a generous sprig of fresh rosemary, leaves picked

    1 litre vegetable stock

    2 x 400g tins of plum tomatoes

    3 sticks of celery, chopped

    2 carrots, peeled and chopped

    a handful of kale, washed and chopped

    1 x 400g tin of cannellini beans, drained

    100g small pasta shells

    a big handful of frozen peas

    a small bunch of fresh basil, chopped

    salt and freshly ground black pepper

    grated Parmesan cheese to serve

Heat a deep saucepan and add a splash of olive oil. Add the onion, garlic, thyme and rosemary and cook gently for 2 to 3 minutes until soft. Pour in the stock and the tomatoes and bring to the boil. Turn the heat down a bit so the soup is simmering gently, then add the celery and carrots and cook for about 15 minutes.

Throw in the chopped kale, the cannellini beans and the pasta and cook for 10 minutes more, then stir in the peas. Bring back to the boil and add the basil. Season with salt and a few twists of pepper, and serve in bowls, sprinkled with Parmesan and drizzle with a bit more olive oil if desired.

With Simon and Clara

Bruschetta

This is a bit of an Italian classic and delicious served as a starter.

Serves 4

    2 cloves of garlic

    4 ripe tomatoes

    extra virgin olive oil

    1 teaspoon balsamic vinegar

    a small bunch of fresh basil

    salt and freshly ground black pepper

    4 slices of good bread

Cut 1 clove of garlic in half and keep one of the halves to one side. Peel the rest of the garlic and slice it all finely. Cut the tomatoes into small chunks and mix them with the sliced garlic, a few glugs of olive oil and the balsamic vinegar. Tear up the basil leaves and stir them in, season with salt and pepper and leave everything to marinate for about half an hour before using to get the best taste.

Toast the bread on both sides either under a hot grill or on a hot griddle pan. Rub the toast quickly with the reserved half clove of garlic, then pile on the topping and serve.

Creamy mushroom, smoked salmon and prawn pasta ☀

Serves 2

olive oil

1 clove of garlic, peeled and chopped

1 small onion, peeled and sliced

100g mushrooms, sliced

100g peeled raw prawns

salt and freshly ground black pepper

140ml single cream

50g grated Parmesan cheese

250g fresh pasta - use whatever you like

100g smoked salmon, torn into strips

a small bunch of fresh basil, leaves picked

Heat a frying pan and add a splash of oil. Add the garlic and onion and cook gently until softened. Throw in the mushrooms and the prawns, season with salt and pepper, then turn the heat up and fry until they start to colour and smell fantastic. Turn the heat down and add the cream and Parmesan. Simmer for a couple of minutes.

Cook the pasta according to the packet instructions, then drain in a colander and stir into the sauce with the strips of smoked salmon. Season with a little salt and pepper, and serve sprinkled with the basil leaves.

When I bought the restaurant I also bought this big, rambling house that I'd fallen in love with. It needed a lot of renovation, and I really enjoyed doing it up, especially the kitchen. In an ideal world I would like a huge kitchen with all the gadgets, but you really only need the basics. You don't need all those fancy tools. In the old days, people didn't have them anyway. In Thailand they don't even use ovens, they just use a pot to stir-fry everything. People put too much emphasis on fancy kitchens. I can get by with a couple of burners and an oven. In the winter, when the restaurant was up and running I would always have people over for dinner. It meant I got to know some of the local people quite well and that made me feel part of the community. There is a really good vibe in my house in France, and it's nice being in the kitchen looking out with the door open. When I bought the property it was as good as derelict, but now the house has a beautiful atmosphere and you can still sense something of its medieval origins. Being in southern Europe, the doors and windows are open in the warmer months and the kitchen becomes almost part of the outside. You can wander down to the lawns and the swimming pool and just take in the view. It's a lovely retreat. I've been renovating the house for four years and it's pretty much finished now, so at last I can sit back and enjoy my summers and relish more experimentation with cooking.

Aubergine and courgette ratatouille ☀

Serves 2 to 4

olive oil

2 medium red onions, peeled and sliced

2 cloves of garlic, peeled and sliced

1 good-sized courgette, diced

1 aubergine, diced

salt and freshly ground black pepper

1/2 a glass of red wine

1 x 400g tin of plum tomatoes

2 fresh jalapeño chillies, chopped

tomato purée

Pour a good glug of oil into a heavy frying pan and add the onion and garlic. Cook for a few minutes, then add the courgette and aubergine with some salt and pepper, and cook for 5 minutes more.

Pour in the wine, cook for another 5 minutes, then add the tomatoes, chillies and a squeeze of tomato purée. Simmer gently for about 10 minutes, stirring now and then and adding a little water if it starts to get a bit too thick.

Taste and add a little more salt and pepper if you need to, then serve.

Queen of puddings

Serves 4

> 4 eggs
>
> 300ml milk
>
> 300ml double cream
>
> 100g white bread or brioche crumbs
>
> 2 tablespoons raspberry jam
>
> 75g caster sugar

Separate 3 of the eggs and put the yolks in one bowl, the whites in another. Try not to get any yolk at all in with the whites, this will stop them whipping up. Break the last egg in with the yolks, add the milk and cream and beat until well mixed together. Stir in the breadcrumbs.

Spread the jam evenly over the bottom of an ovenproof baking dish and pour the mixture over the top. Set your oven to 150°C/300°F/gas mark 2, and leave the pudding to stand for 30 minutes while it heats up. Bake the pudding in the preheated oven for an hour, until set.

In a clean bowl, whisk the egg whites until stiff, fold in the sugar and spoon on top of the cooked pudding. Sprinkle with a little more sugar and carefully replace in the oven for a further 15 – 20 minutes, until the meringue is golden brown and cooked through.

Gina's fruits of the forest

Gina uses kirsch for this recipe but it's quite hard to get hold of. If you can't find it, use cointreau or grand marnier or any type of fruity liquer.

Serves 4 to 6

> 600ml double cream
>
> 450g mixed ripe red fruits – strawberries, raspberries, blackberries, red or blackcurrants
>
> 3 tablespoons kirsch
>
> 1 tablespoon sugar

Pour the cream into a mixing bowl and whisk until thick. Pick through the fruit, removing any stalks or green tops, and put a handful of the nicest ones to one side. Whiz the rest in a blender or food processor with the kirsch and the sugar.

Fold the whizzed fruit into the cream, then pour into some clean dessert glasses or bowls. Chill in the fridge for an hour, and decorate with the reserved fruit before serving.

272

In the village beside my house they have these country fairs. A lot of the area is farmland, and the community has a great connection with the land, the seasons and the produce – and how to get the most affordable healthy food from it. So every year they get together to eat and drink, and share their produce. Everyone mucks in. I remember going to one of the fêtes, it was after their *chasse*, which is like the hunting season. I think that was the first time I tried wild boar. It was delicious. It was local peasant cooking – really good food. It almost reminded me of the stews we used to have when I was growing up. The process of cooking for these fêtes is fascinating to watch, because they cater for the whole community and all the surrounding farmlands. It involves many generations, young and old. There is a production line of

preparing, cooking and serving. Everyone donates produce from their farms: meat, vegetables, whatever fruit is in season. It is a community thing, so they all muck in, and just enjoy the day together.

The central dish is like a casserole stew, and this is served up with lovely fresh bread which they make on the spot in fantastic portable bread ovens that are brought on a cart on the back of a tractor. People sit together for ages eating and talking and actually take their time. We all too often have that thing about food – grab a burger, get it down. Grab an ice-cream, get it down. Rush every-thing, like it's something to be got over with. It's not a healthy way to eat. We can learn a lot from the way people who live and eat from the land take time over their food, and that's what I'll always remember about my times in France..

French farmers' fair chicken stew

Serves 4

    4 medium potatoes, peeled and cut into chunks

    20ml olive oil

    1 x 1.5kg/3lb chicken, cut into 8 pieces

    4 carrots, peeled and cut into large chunks

    2 stalks of celery, chopped

    3 cloves of garlic, peeled and chopped

    200ml dry white wine

    500ml chicken stock

    1 bouquet garni

    2 heads of chicory, quartered lengthwise

    salt and freshly ground black pepper

Cook the potatoes in boiling water for 5 minutes and drain.

Heat the oil in a large pan and fry the chicken pieces until well browned. Add the carrots, celery and garlic and fry for a further 2 minutes. Deglaze the pan with the white wine and leave to sizzle for 1 minute. Add the chicken stock and bouquet garni and cook for another 10 minutes on a medium heat.

Remove the bouquet garni at this point if you don't want the flavour of the herbs to be too strong, and add the potatoes. Season with salt and pepper and simmer until the potatoes are tender and the chicken is cooked through. Add the quartered chicory. When the chicory has wilted, remove the chicken and arrange in a serving dish. Spoon over the sauce and the vegetables and serve.

French farmers' fair doughnuts

150g sugar

5 eggs

1/2 litre milk

250g butter

75g easy-blend yeast

½ teaspoon vanilla essence

1.75kg flour

20g salt

sunflower oil

Place the sugar and the eggs in a large bowl and either whisk or use an electric mixer to blend thoroughly. Add the milk and butter to the bowl and continue to whisk until smooth and creamy. Stir in the yeast and vanilla, then add the flour and salt and beat until you have a nice thick consistency.

Heat the oil in a large pan until it's very hot. Drop a large tablespoon of the batter into the oil and fry for 3 minutes, until lightly browned on both sides. Remove from the pan and drain on kitchen paper. Sprinkle with caster sugar and serve.

I'm still involved in acting and will probably continue to be, but in the long run, having worked solidly for so long, I'm thinking about having more space to enjoy myself, planning the year around working some months and travelling and exploring during the remainder. There are so many parts of the world I've yet to discover, and I need to arrange my life to have enough gaps to be able to do that.

For me, cooking has always been about sharing with friends and family and learning about different cultures through the food that people eat. Enjoying a meal prepared from the freshest ingredients and put together simply, with those you're closest to beats any kind of fancy restaurant.

Cooking is not just for trained chefs, or for people with loads of spare time on their hands, and it doesn't have to have to cost much or involve obscure types of ingredients from specialist shops. Anyone can do it.

What I hope I've managed to get across in this book is just how uncomplicated cooking can be and how, once you've started, it can become a lasting passion. I get a lot of contentment from cooking and from the ongoing learning processes that it can involve. And more than that, I think it's a great way of finding out about different countries, meeting new people and forging lifelong friendships.

Conversion chart

Weight		Oven Temperature			Volume	
10g	0.5 oz	Gas mark 1	140°C	275°F	2fl oz	55ml
20g	0.75 oz	Gas mark 2	150°C	300°F	3fl oz	75ml
25g	1 oz	Gas mark 3	170°C	325°F	4fl oz	110ml
50g	2 oz	Gas mark 4	180°C	350°F	5fl oz	140ml
100g	4 oz	Gas mark 5	190°C	375°F	6fl oz	170ml
150g	5 oz	Gas mark 6	200°C	400°F	7fl oz	200ml
200g	7 oz	Gas mark 7	220°C	425°F	8fl oz	230ml
250g	9 oz	Gas mark 8	230°C	450°F	9fl oz	260ml
300g	11 oz	Gas mark 9	240°C	475°F	10fl oz	285ml
350g	12 oz					
400g	14 oz					
450g	1 lb					
550g	1.25 lb					
750g	1.5 lb					
1 kg	2 lb 3 oz					

Index